D1539172

Wildflowers and Waterfalls

of Western New England

and Eastern New York

Phyllis Pryzby

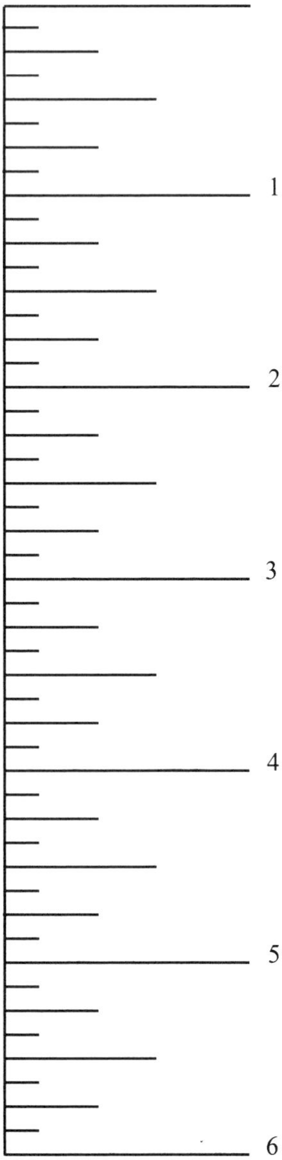
1
2
3
4
5
6

Wildflowers and Waterfalls

of Western New England

and Eastern New York

by Phyllis Pryzby

Photographs by the Author

ISBN 0-9700509-3-3

Due to changes in conditions, use of
the information in this book is at the
sole risk of the user.

Published by Phyllis Pryzby

Printed in the United States of America by
The Studley Press
Dalton, Massachusetts

This book is dedicated to my husband, John, whose help made it possible for this book to be published.

CONTENTS

WILDFLOWER PHOTOGRAPHS

WATERFALL PHOTOGRAPHS

INTRODUCTION

From The Author

There are wonderful wildflowers and waterfalls in western New England and eastern New York. This book will show where to find the waterfalls and where and when to see the wildflowers blooming. Waterfalls and wildflowers are a joy to behold and take only time, some effort, and a little expense to see. I will begin with some information about waterfalls.

Information about Waterfalls

Waterfalls do not always look the same. They are very dependent on the weather. Some waterfalls look nice, but just not as full, in dry weather. However, others have very little water unless there is a good rainfall. I have mentioned this in the *What to Expect* section if I considered it important.

To find a waterfall at its peak, go in the spring or a day or two after a rainfall (three or four if it was a heavy rain.) Waterfalls that are in a valley below mountains are likely to have a lot of water for a longer time after it has rained than waterfalls that are not in a valley.

Photographs of Waterfalls

Photographs of the waterfalls listed in this book can be found after the wildflower pictures. They have been divided by states and arranged alphabetically within each state. They are listed in the index with their number and state abbreviation in bold text. For example: Kent Falls **3CT**.

Photographing Waterfalls

Taking a good picture of a waterfall can be a rewarding experience. The main thing to keep in mind is that waterfalls have movement, so most people like to see a picture that shows this movement. To do this, the picture should be taken at a fairly slow shutter speed (1/15th of a second to 1/4th of a second or possibly even slower). Many people need to use a tripod to get pictures at these speeds. Don't be afraid to experiment and find your own preference and abilities.

It is also helpful to have a zoom lens so you can take pictures of waterfalls of different sizes and from various distances.

I used 200 speed film for most of the waterfall photographs in this book. I took most of the pictures at a shutter speed of 1/4th of a second.

Photographs of waterfalls in the woods often have blotches of light if taken on a sunny day. Therefore, you might prefer cloudy or at least partly cloudy days for waterfall photography in woodlands.

Wildflowers Along Trails to Waterfalls

You will notice that some of the places that have lists of wildflowers are along the trails to waterfalls. My experience has been that many people who like waterfalls also like wildflowers and vice versa. Therefore, when I hiked to a waterfall, I made lists of the wildflowers that were blooming along the way.

I found that some places had many wildflowers near the trail to a waterfall, so I decided to go to those places several times to get lists of the wildflowers that bloomed at various times. The trails to some other waterfalls had few flowers, so I went to those only once or twice.

During the summer, I hiked some woodland trails to waterfalls. I found few or no wildflowers blooming along the trails since it was Summer, but I listed some wildflower plants that would bloom in the Spring or Fall. I specified that these flowers were not blooming by adding (leaves), (gone to seed), (buds), (berries), etc. after the plant name.

Ways To Use This Book

To find waterfalls that are open to the public in western New England and eastern New York.

To look at and enjoy pictures of waterfalls in these areas.

To discover where and when you can find specific wildflowers blooming along trails that are open to the public.

To look at and enjoy pictures of various wildflowers that grow and bloom in western New England and eastern New York.

To learn the names of wildflowers that can be found in western New England and eastern New York.

To determine which flowers bloom in the woods and which bloom in fields.

How I Developed My Lists of Wildflowers

I gathered the wildflower lists for this book by hiking along various trails open to the public. As I walked, I wrote down each flower the first time I saw it blooming and usually never listed it again on that trail. The exception to that rule would be at Norcross Wildlife Sanctuary. Since there are many wildflower areas there, and people can choose which areas to view, I often listed all the flowers I saw in *each* area.

Sometimes I named certain landmarks along a trail and then listed more wildflowers found after the landmarks. This was to break up parts of the trail, show what a hiker would see besides wildflowers, and to show how far one would have to go to see certain flowers. After the landmark I would list the flowers I had not seen before on that trail.

Because wildflowers bloom throughout the season along trails that have both sunny and shady areas, I hiked that type of trail twice a month. However, since very few wildflowers bloom in woodlands in the Summer, I rarely hiked those areas at that time.

Meaning of "Beginning, Middle, and End" of Each Month

In my wildflower lists, each month is divided into three sections - beginning of the month, middle of the month, and end of the month. The beginning of the month is the 1st through the 10th day, the middle of the month is the 11th through the 20th day, and the end of the month is the 21st through the 31st day.

Early and Late Seasons

I noticed that some flowers bloomed earlier some years and later in others, especially in Spring. Late seasons seemed to occur as a result of cold spring weather or a late snowfall. I have noted at the beginning of my lists whether I obtained my information during an early or late season. With this information the reader can try to optimize his or her chances of finding the flowers blooming. If interested in finding specific flowers blooming, try to notice whether the Spring is early or late.

Conditions that May Vary from Year to Year, Time to Time, and Place to Place.

When I wrote my first two books *Wildflowers of the Berkshires Where and When They Bloom Vol. 1 and Vol. 2*, I walked the same trails at least twice a month during both an early season and a late season, making lists of what was blooming each time. I noticed that I saw a few flowers blooming one year and not the next. I gave various reasons why that might occur, but suffice it to say that there may be some variations in the wildflowers that bloom from year to year.

I have also noticed a variation in the shades of flower colors. The shade of a flower depends on various elements such as the amount of light they receive, soil conditions, and whether the bloom has just opened or is ready to fade. Therefore, do not be concerned if the flower you are looking at has a slightly different shade than what is shown in this book.

Entrance or parking fees may vary from year to year.

Preservation of Flower Species

I hope my readers will resist the urge to pick the flowers or dig out the plants they see, especially the unusual ones. If flowers are picked, plants cannot produce seeds for reproduction.

Mowing an area before flowering plants have been able to produce their seeds also has a negative effect on plant reproduction. When an area is mowed, plants often try to continue their cycle and sometimes produce their flowers and seeds later. Some, however, don't have a chance to do this before the growing season has ended.

Annuals (plants that live only one year) and biennials (plants that live two years, produce flowers and seeds only the second year, and then die) are especially vulnerable to extinction from an area since they depend exclusively on seed production for propagation.

Attempts to transplant wildflowers may kill many of them, either because conditions in the new area are not conducive to their growth, or because they are extremely difficult to transplant. Therefore, I am hoping my readers will enjoy the flowers they see, but leave them where they are growing. Taking wildflowers from their natural habitats will also make it impossible for other hikers to enjoy them.

If any of my readers are interested in growing wildflowers in their own garden, the New England Wildflower Society sells both wildflower seeds and plants and provides directions about how to grow them.

Their address is:

New England Wild Flower Society, Inc.
Garden in the Woods
180 Hemenway Road
Framingham, MA 01701-2699

Their website is: www.newfs.org

Flower Listing and Sources of Flower Names

I used *Newcomb's Wildflower Guide* by Lawrence Newcomb as my primary source for wildflower names which are listed by their common names. In cases where there is more than one common name, the flowers are listed in the order given in Newcomb's book with the second and/or third name in brackets. For example: Pink Azalea [Pinxter Flower] means Pink Azalea is the first name and Pinxter Flower is the second name given in Newcomb's book. Cow [Tufted] Vetch means Newcomb's book has it listed as Cow or Tufted Vetch. This means it can be called Cow Vetch or Tufted Vetch. False [White] Hellebore [Indian Poke] means this plant can be called False Hellebore, White Hellebore, or Indian Poke.

The flowers listed in this book are only those I personally saw blooming. The lists may not be totally comprehensive, but will be accurate to what I saw on my walks. Since there is a fine line between garden flowers and wildflowers, I included the garden perennials, trees, and shrubs that I saw blooming along the trails in my lists as well as wildflowers.

I used the *Encyclopedia of Flowers* published by Fog City Press in San Francisco, CA as my main source for garden perennial names. The Audubon Society *Field Guide to North*

American Trees was my source for the names of trees. A few flowers that I could not find in any book have not been listed.

The wildflowers that I saw at Norcross Wildlife Sanctuary include the names given in Newcomb's book and also the names given at Norcross if they were different. I usually, but not always, listed the names given in Newcomb's book first. There were flowers at Norcross that were not listed in Newcomb's book, so those are only listed by the names given at Norcross.

For those with a knowledge of scientific names, I have included two indices - one of scientific names with their common name equivalents and another of common names with their scientific name equivalents.

To give a picture of what a visitor might expect, I often commented on the flowers I saw in a certain area. These comments are surrounded by parentheses. Examples are (many), (few), (beginning to bloom), etc.

I have not listed some wildflowers that are very common or very small. These are Common Dandelion, Black Medick, Hop [Yellow] Clover, Low Hop Clover, Least Hop Clover, White Clover, Wild Madder, Garlic Mustard, Horseweed, and Mouse-ear Chickweed.

To simplify the lists, I did not mention the species of some genera. Goldenrods, for instance, have been lumped together with the exception of Zigzag [Broad-leaved] Goldenrod, Blue-stemmed [Wreath] Goldenrod, and Silverrod. Similarly, Violets have been differentiated only by color of flower except Dame's Violet. The species of Blue-eyed Grass and Buttercups were not mentioned.

Wildflower Photographs

I brought my camera on most walks and took pictures of the flowers I observed. Many of these pictures are included in this book to aid in identification. They are listed in the index in bold type.

Size and Arrangement of Flower Pictures

The size of the flowers of each species varies somewhat, but stays within certain parameters. The pictures in this book indicate the approximate size of each flower by the size of the picture and a size indicator written at the right of the flower name. The size indicators tell how large the picture is compared with the flower. One example would be (x 1/2) which would mean that the picture is half as large as the flower. Another would be (x 2/5) meaning that that the flower picture is 2/5ths as large as the flower.

The pictures in this book are organized by the shapes of the flowers and arrangement of the leaves.

Explanation of Terms Used to Describe Shapes of Flowers

Regular flowers: Flowers that have petals or petal-like parts that are similar to each other in shape, size, and color and are arranged around the center like spokes of a wheel. If the petals are united, as in bell-shaped flowers, they are considered regular if the lobes (outer rounded parts) are similar in shape, size, and color.

Some flowers with regular parts have petals that are somewhat divided and can appear to have more petals than they do. Examples would be shapes like:

or

Therefore, in determining the number of petals, one must observe them from their point of origin. A magnifying glass often helps to do this.

Irregular flowers: Flowers that are <u>not</u> radially symmetrical. Their petals or petal-like parts are <u>not</u> similar in shape, size, or color.

Indistinguishable flowers: Flowers that have no noticeable petal-like parts or have parts so small that their numbers or arrangement is difficult to discern. Be aware, however, that some flowers may have parts that are recognizable if seen under a magnifying glass, so they may be listed by the shape and number of petals even though appearing indistinguishable to the naked eye.

Explanation of Terms Used to Describe the Arrangement of Leaves

<u>Note</u>: When trying to determine the arrangement of leaves on the main stem, observe an area where the leaves are widely spaced so their arrangement is distinct.

Basal leaves only: Leaves growing only from the base of the plant.

Stem leaves: Leaves growing on the main stem of the plant.

Opposite leaves: Leaves growing directly across from each other on the main stem.

Example:

<u>Caution</u>: Some plants have what appear to be secondary stems branching from the main stem with leaves on each branch. The apparent leaves are opposite each other on this secondary stem. This stem may even divide again into two opposite stems. This arrangement can be misinterpreted as being opposite leaves. However, if their connection to the main stem is alternate, not opposite, they are considered to be divided leaves with several leaflets arranged alternately on the main stem.

Four examples of two divided [segmented] leaves arranged alternately on the main stem:

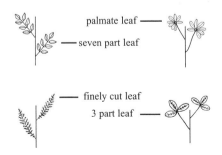

palmate leaf ———

——— seven part leaf

——— finely cut leaf

3 part leaf ———

Whorled leaves: Leaves growing in circles of three or more around the main stem in one or more places on the stem.

Alternate leaves: Leaves arranged singly (not opposite) on the main stem. Leaves vary in shape and can be either simple or divided.

Examples:

General Shapes of Leaves

There is a wide variety of shapes in leaves. Some have straight edges, some are toothed, some are lobed, and some are divided with several leaflets (see the four examples on the previous page.) However, I am including only information about shapes of leaves that is necessary for use in this book.

Heart-shaped leaves: Leaves in the shape of a valentine heart.

Example:

Lance-shaped leaves: Leaves that are wider at one end and narrow to a point at the other end, usually three or more times longer than wide.

Examples of lance-shaped leaves mentioned in the picture section:

Narrowly lance-shaped

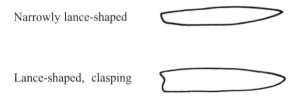

Lance-shaped, clasping

Clasping leaves (leaves that clasp stem): Leaves that begin directly at the stem and surround the stem part way.

Example:

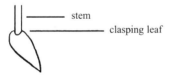

Explanation of Unusually-shaped Stem

Winged stem: The stem that joins the leaf to the main stem is wider than usual. Lowrie's Aster is identified by a winged stem.

Example:

 winged stem —

Acknowledgements

I received help from many people whom I would like to thank. I owe the most to my husband, John, who did the computer work for the pictures and covers. He assisted me in entering the information into the computer, gave me suggestions and encouragement, edited and formatted some of the book, and prepared it for printing.

I would also like to express my appreciation to my sister, Marion Thompson, who accompanied me on most of my trips to find wildflowers and waterfalls and also helped me in many ways.

I would like to thank Leslie Duthie of Norcross Wildlife Sanctuary, Alec Gillman of Mount Greylock State Reservation, and Ron Wolanin from the Massachusetts Audubon Society for the information they gave me about their respective areas.

I would also like to express my appreciation to the Friends of the Railroad Run and those that helped them for enhancing the beauty of the area by planting bulbs and wildflowers in the median strip.

DRIVING DIRECTIONS, WHAT TO EXPECT, AND TRAIL INFORMATION

Connecticut

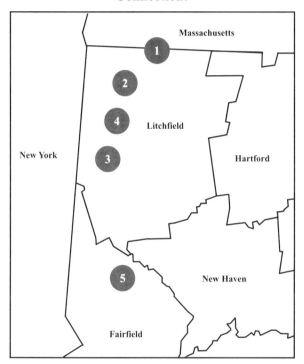

1. Campbells Falls - North Norfolk, CT & Southfield, MA
2. Dean's Ravine - Canaan, CT
3. Kent Falls - Kent, CT
4. Pine Swamp Brook Falls - Sharon, CT
5. Prydden Brook Falls - Newtown, CT

1 Campbells Falls

Campbells Falls State Park
North Norfolk, CT   Litchfield County and
Southfield, MA   Berkshire County

See Picture No.39CT.

<u>Driving Directions from Great Barrington, Massachusetts</u>:
Take Route 23 East from the Route 7 and Route 23 intersection, which is east of the center of Great Barrington. Drive 3.5 miles and then go right onto Route 57 East. After driving 5.8 miles on Route 57 East (and 183 South), turn right onto New Marlboro Southfield Road. (There is a sign there saying "Southfield, Canaan, CT.") Stay on the New Marlboro Southfield Road for 1.3 miles. (Do not turn right at Kolburn School.) At 1.3 miles there will be a fork in the road with writing on the fence pointing to the left for "Southfield - Norfolk Rt. 272." Turn left and go over a metal grate bridge. Drive 4.6 miles through and past Southfield. There are two signs for Campbells Falls State Park - one in Southfield pointing straight ahead and another pointing to the right. Follow both signs. The road after the right turn is not paved, but you will find the State Forest in 0.4 miles. There is a small unpaved parking area to the left.

There is a field that is part of Campbells Falls State Park that can be reached by car by going past the second sign for Campbells Falls State Park and turning right on Tobey Hill Road. Drive 0.1 miles on this road and you will find the field on the right.

<u>Driving Directions from Connecticut</u>: Drive north on State Road 272 towards the Massachusetts border. Look for Elmore Road on the right (past Ginger Creek Nursery). Continue straight 1.1 miles and pass Tobey Hill Road on the left. Go 0.2 miles further and turn left onto the unpaved Campbells Falls State Park Road. Drive 0.4 miles on Campbells Falls State Park Road to the small unpaved parking area on the left for Campbells Falls State Park.

<u>What to Expect</u>: Besides a nice waterfall, Campbells Falls State Park has some very nice wildflowers in the Spring and Summer. I went there five times to discover which wildflowers were blooming, as well as to see the falls.

Campbells Falls does not require extremely wet weather to look good as some other waterfalls do. However, extremely dry weather will have a negative effect on its volume. On the other hand, wet weather makes the trails muddy and possibly slippery, so wear boots in wet weather. Stay on the trails and watch for Poison Ivy. There are some mosquitoes and small biting black flies, but not a lot.

The field mentioned in the trail information has a picnic table and a pit toilet. However, the pit toilet was often closed off when I was there. There is no entrance fee.

<u>Trail Information</u>:   Campbells Falls State Park straddles Massachusetts and Connecticut. The parking lot is in Massachusetts and the falls are in Connecticut.

From the Campbells Falls parking lot you will see two trails. The one going down goes to the falls. The trail to the falls has occasional trail blazes on trees. This trail is somewhat steep in places.

The trail consists of soil, stones, roots, pine needles and leaves which might be slippery, especially in wet weather, so wear hiking boots. The falls are not hard to find because you will hear them and then see them fairly soon. The trail to the falls is about 0.1 miles from the parking lot.

Just before arriving at the falls, there is a short trail to the left. I usually turned onto that trail to discover what wildflowers were blooming there. This side trail takes about 10 minutes to hike round trip.

The trail to the left of the parking lot (looking from the road) goes through woods, over several bridges, and to a field that has many beautiful wildflowers during the end of May and beginning of June. The entrance to this field is often somewhat wet. This trail is marked by square yellow markers on trees. It will take approximately 22 minutes round trip if walked at a medium speed without stopping.

The field at the end of this trail can also be reached by car. (See Driving Directions.)

Nearby Waterfalls and Trails with Wildflowers listed in this book: Dean's Ravine Falls in Canaan, Pine Swamp Brook Falls in Sharon, and Kent Falls in Kent (all in Connecticut); also Harlem Valley Rail Trail in Millerton, NY; and Bash Bish Falls in Mt. Washington, Massachusetts

Nearby Trails with Wildflowers listed in my books *Wildflowers of the Berkshires Where and When They Bloom Vol. 1 and Vol. 2*: Fountain Pond in Great Barrington, Tyringham Cobble in Tyringham, and Bartholomew's Cobble in Sheffield (all in Vol. 1); also Benedict Pond (Beartown State Forest) in Great Barrington and Monterey (Vol. 2) All of these are in Massachusetts.

2 Dean's Ravine

Housatonic State Forest
Canaan, Connecticut   Litchfield County

See Picture No. 40CT.

Driving Directions (from the North): On Route 7 South go through Canaan. Continue on Route 7 past the junction with Route 126. From that junction continue 1.6 miles on Route 7 and then turn left onto Lime Rock Station Road. Drive 1 mile and then turn left onto Music Mountain Road. Go 0.8 miles and look for a parking area on the left. When I was there, there was a place for a sign, but there was no sign.

Driving Directions (from the South): Take Route 7 North from West Cornwall. After a junction with Route 112 continue 0.3 miles on Route 7. Then turn right onto Lime Rock Station Road. Drive 1 mile and turn left onto Music Mountain Road. Go 0.8 miles and look for a parking area on the left. When I was there, there was a place for a sign, but there was no sign.

What to Expect: Dean's Ravine consists basically of a parking lot, a trail through the woods, and a waterfall. The waterfall is part of Reed Brook. The water goes sideways and down along rocks most of the way rather than straight down. There are no rest rooms and no fees.

Trail Information: The trail to the falls begins at the left side of the parking lot. It generally goes downhill to the falls and is marked by light blue blazes on trees. Near the falls you will see double blue blazes on the left. The trail continues straight and also goes sharply right. Take the sharp right. The trail is steeper from this point to the falls. There is another tree with double blue blazes. Turn left there. The distance from the parking lot to the falls is about 0.4 miles.

Nearby Waterfalls and Trails with Wildflowers listed in this book: Pine Swamp Brook Falls in Sharon, Kent Falls in Kent, and Campbells Falls in North Norfolk (all in Connecticut); also Bash Bish Falls in Mount Washington, Massachusetts; and Harlem Valley Rail Trail in Millerton, New York

Nearby Trails with Wildflowers listed in my books *Wildflowers of the Berkshires Where and When They Bloom Vol. 1 and Vol. 2*: Bartholomew's Cobble in Sheffield and Fountain Pond in Great Barrington (both in Vol. 1); also Benedict Pond (Beartown State Forest) in Great Barrington and Monterey (Vol. 2). All are in Massachusetts.

3 Kent Falls

Kent Falls State Park
Kent, Connecticut   Litchfield County

See Picture No. 41CT.

Driving Directions from the North: Kent Falls is on Route 7 north of the business district of Kent. Travel south on Route 7 from Cornwall Bridge toward Kent. Route 4 joins Route 7 for a short distance and then they separate. Continue 3.9 miles on Route 7 South past this separation point to find Kent Falls State Park. The park is also 0.3 miles south of the sign for the Kent town line. There are signs for Kent Falls State Park on both sides of the highway. The park is on the left. You can see the falls from the highway as you approach from the north. Turn left into a large parking lot.

<u>Driving directions from the South</u>: Take Route 7 north to Kent, Connecticut. From the intersection of Route 7 North and Route 341 continue north on Route 7 for about 5.3 miles where you will find Kent Falls State Park. There will be a sign and you can also see the lower falls to the right. Turn right into a large parking lot.

<u>What to Expect</u>: Kent Falls State Park has two major waterfalls and several cascades. One waterfall can be seen from the highway as mentioned in the directions. The other one can be seen to the left of the Kent Falls Trail.

Kent Falls State Park has a large black-top parking lot. To get to the falls and the park itself you have to cross the Kent Falls Brook. There are two foot bridges to do this - one covered bridge and one bridge with a railing. Beyond the bridges is a large mowed area with picnic tables, a black-top sidewalk, fountain, and modern rest rooms. The rest rooms are open from mid-May into October. There is also a pit toilet that can be used before and after those dates.

There are some nice wildflowers beyond the mowed area, especially near the brook, in the Summer. In fact, the wildflowers were so nice that I went to Kent Falls nine times to get lists of the flowers blooming in the area for those who are interested in wildflowers as well as waterfalls.

The park opens at 8AM and closes at sunset. Pets should be on a leash no longer than 7 feet and under the control of their owner. No swimming is allowed at Kent Falls.

There is no fee at times. However, there is a charge for parking on weekends and holidays from May through October. It is $7 for Connecticut residents and $10 for out of state cars.

Trail Information: When I was at Kent Falls, I walked over the wooden bridge with railings, up a blacktop sidewalk, and continued to the left near the edge of the woods. Most of the lawn was mowed, but I walked on the edge of the mowed area at this point and had an unmowed area to my right. This unmowed area often had wildflowers.

After that, I came to the Kent Falls Trail. This trail is quite an upward climb. It is 1/4 mile long and the vertical climb is 250 feet. There are square wooden logs for steps part of the way. Other parts of the trail have rocks, soil, and roots. There is a wooden railing beside the steps most of the way.

There are lookouts at the Kent Falls Brook. In some places you can see cascades, and near the top you can see the upper falls pictured in this book. There were several other trails in the area, but I stayed on the trail near the Kent Falls Brook. The Kent Falls Trail takes about 25 minutes round trip if you walk at a medium speed without stopping.

After I went back down the Kent Falls Trail, I turned right, went down some steps toward the lower falls, and then turned left to follow the Kent Falls Brook downstream. There is a blacktop sidewalk going down to a covered bridge. I went down near the edge of the mowed area, listing flowers to the right of this area and near the brook. I usually turned left before the covered bridge and continued on the left side of the brook. Then I returned to the parking lot via the wooden bridge with hand railings.

Occasionally I varied my walk, but the wildflower lists will reflect this variation.

Nearby Waterfalls and Trails with Wildflowers listed in this book: Pine Swamp Brook Falls in Sharon and Dean's Ravine Falls in Canaan (both in Connecticut); also Harlem Valley Rail Trail in Millerton, New York; and Bash Bish Falls in Mount Washington, Massachusetts

Nearby Trails with Wildflowers listed in my book *Wildflowers of the Berkshires   Where and When They Bloom   Vol. 1*: Bartholomew's Cobble in Sheffield, Massachusetts

4 Pine Swamp Brook Falls

Sharon, Connecticut   Litchfield County

See Picture No. 42CT.

Driving Directions from the North: From Canaan take Route 7 South. When Route 128 goes left, continue on Route 7 for 0.2 miles where you will find a pull-off on the right.   Just beyond that pull-off, you will see the falls to the right of the highway.   The falls are on the inside of a curve, so many people pass it without being aware that it exists.

Driving Directions from the South: Take Route 7 North from Kent or North Kent. You will see a sign for the Sharon Town Line on the right. The falls are 3.9 miles from the Sharon sign. There are about 3 small pull-off areas near the falls (all on the left). The falls are easy to miss as they are on the inside of a curve in the highway. They are just to the left of a small bridge.

What to Expect: This waterfall has two separate drops. The total drop is about 30 feet. After the falls, the water goes under the highway and into the Housatonic River.

Trail Information: There is no trail since the falls are right beside the highway.

Nearby Waterfalls and Trails with Wildflowers listed in this book: Kent Falls in Kent, Dean's Ravine Falls in Canaan (both in Connecticut); Campbells Falls in North Norfolk, Connecticut and Southfield, Massachusetts; also Harlem Valley Rail Trail in Millerton, New York; and Bash Bish Falls in Mount Washington, Massachusetts

Nearby Trails with Wildflowers listed in my book *Wildflowers of the Berkshires   Where and When They Bloom   Vol. 1*: Bartholomew's Cobble in Sheffield, Massachusetts

5 *Prydden Brook Falls*

Paugusett State Forest
Newtown, Connecticut   Fairfield County

See Picture No. 43CT.

Driving Directions from Highway I-84 West of Newtown: Take Exit 11 off I-84. The distance from the this exit to Great Quarter Road is 5 miles.

At the end of the exit road, follow the signs to Route 34 East. Then follow 34 East to Great Quarter Road on the left. Follow Great Quarter Road about 1.3 miles to its end at a cul-de-sac. There you will find a parking lot for the Paugusett State Forest.

<u>What to Expect</u>: Prydden Brook Falls is a very picturesque waterfall. The main waterfall pictured in this book is about 25 feet high. This is not as large as some other waterfalls, but it forms several cascades, making a lovely picture. Below the main falls are several other cascades, but the upper area is the most artistic.

There were very few wildflowers along the trail in June, but it was a little late for woodland flowers to bloom. Therefore, I listed some of the plants that would have bloomed earlier. Some of the trail is deep woods, so wildflowers will not be abundant, but the falls are definitely worth the trip.

Be aware that hunting is allowed, so wear bright clothing in the fall. There were only a few mosquitoes. There are no rest rooms and there is no fee.

<u>Trail Information</u>: Prydden Brook Falls can be reached by walking about 1.5 miles along the Zoar Trail. This trail begins just to the right of a bulletin board beside the parking lot. It is marked with blue blazes on trees.

This trail goes near the shore of Lake Zoar, a dammed-up area of the Housatonic River. The trail is level in some places and goes up and down in others - sometimes gently and occasionally it is fairly steep.

The trail crossed four small, thin brooks before reaching Prydden Brook Falls. They were easy to cross by stepping on a few stones. These brooks may dry up in dry weather.

After walking about 1.5 miles, the hiker can hear and also see part of Prydden Brook Falls to the right of Zoar trail. The falls can be viewed from the bottom by hiking down an unmarked trail to the right of Zoar trail. Zoar trail continues after the waterfall, so keep your eyes and ears alert.

The trip to and from the falls can be walked in about 2 1/4 hours if walking at a moderate speed without stopping.

Massachusetts

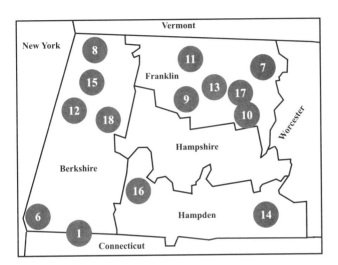

1. Campbells Falls - Southfield, MA/North Norfolk, CT
6. Bash Bish Falls - Mount Washington, MA
7. Bear's Den Falls - New Salem, MA
8. Cascade Falls - North Adams, MA
9. Chapelbrook Falls - South Ashfield, MA
10. Gunn Brook Falls - Sunderland, MA
11. High Ledges Wildlife Sanctuary - Shelburne, MA
12. Mt. Greylock Reservation - Cheshire/New Ashford, MA
13. Mt. Sugarloaf Reservation - South Deerfield, MA
14. Norcross Wildlife Sanctuary - Monson/Wales, MA
15. Pecks Brook Falls - Adams, MA
16. Sanderson Brook Falls - Chester/Blandford, MA
17. Slatestone Brook Falls - Sunderland, MA
18. Wahconah Falls - Dalton, MA

6 Bash Bish Falls

Bash Bish Falls State Park
Mount Washington, Massachusetts   Berkshire County

See Picture No. 44MA.

<u>Driving Directions from the North</u>: In eastern New York State take Route 22 South to Hillsdale, New York where Route 23 crosses Route 22. From this intersection continue 4.1 miles on Route 22 South and look for Route 344 on the left. Take that turn and follow Route 344, going left a second time. Almost immediately after a sign for Taconic State Park, there will be two signs for Bash Bish. The second sign will have an arrow pointing to the left. Take that left fork and drive 0.6 miles where you will find a parking lot for Bash Bish on the right. The trail to the falls begins at the left of the parking lot if you look with your back to the road.

<u>Driving Directions from the South</u>: Take Route 22 North into Millerton where Route 44 joins Route 22 North. Continue on Route 22 North and 44 East. When Route 44 East separates from 22 North, stay on Route 22 North. From that point go about 12.6 miles and then turn right onto Route 344. Follow Route 344 to the right again and you will soon see a sign for Taconic State Park. Almost immediately after that sign, there will be two signs for Bash Bish. The second sign will have an arrow pointing to the left. Take that left fork and drive 0.6 miles where you will find a parking lot for Bash Bish on the right. The trail to the falls begins at the left of the parking lot if you look with your back to the road.

<u>What to Expect</u>:   Bash Bish Falls is in Massachusetts. However, the parking lot and part of the trail are in New York State. The falls are not only lovely, but also quite large. The falls begin with several smaller waterfalls leading to two large divided waterfalls. The total drop is about 80 feet. There are several cascades below the main waterfalls.

I found there were quite a few Spring wildflowers blooming near the trail, so I went three times to get lists of which flowers were blooming at different times as well at to see the falls.

There is a self-composting outdoor toilet at the end of the trail near the falls. It is usually open from Memorial Day to Columbus Day. There are also rest rooms with flush toilets in the Taconic State Park, which you pass before coming to Bash Bish. Across the street from the entrance to Taconic State Park is a store called the Depot Deli which has a portable toilet to the left of the store.

No swimming is allowed at Bash Bish and there is no fee. No parking is allowed in the parking lot from dusk to 8 AM.

<u>Trail Information</u>: Since many people go to Bash Bish Falls, the trail from the parking lot to the falls is fairly wide and quite worn. Thus there is no need for markers. The trail is made of soil, rocks, leaves, and roots, which may be slippery in wet weather. Be sure to stay on the path because there is Poison Ivy in places.

The trail starts by going slightly downhill for a little while, but soon it changes and goes uphill. It continues uphill (but not steeply) to the falls. Eventually, the path becomes much higher than the Bash Bish Brook. There are wide steps with a metal handrail from the path to the bottom of the falls.

Nearby Waterfalls and Trails with Wildflowers listed in this book: Harlem Valley Rail Trail in Millerton, New York; Dean's Ravine Falls in Canaan, Pine Brook Falls in Sharon, and Kent Falls in Kent (all in Connecticut); also Campbells Falls in North Norfolk, Connecticut and Southfield, Massachusetts.

Nearby Trails with Wildflowers listed in my books *Wildflowers of the Berkshires Where and When They Bloom Vol. 1* and *Vol. 2*: Fountain Pond in Great Barrington and Bartholomew's Cobble in Sheffield (Vol. 1); also Benedict Pond (Beartown State Forest) in Great Barrington (Vol. 2). All are in Massachusetts.

7 Bear's Den Falls

Bear's Den Reservation
New Salem, Massachusetts   Franklin County

See Picture No. 45MA.

Driving Directions from Route 2 West of New Salem: Take Exit 15 off Route 2 East, then take Route 122 South. Soon Route 202 South will join 122 South. In about 0.9 miles they will separate. Continue on 202 South 0.4 miles and then turn right onto Elm Street. Go 0.7 miles and turn left onto Neilson Road. There will be two pull-off areas on the right. Park in the second pull-off area (0.5 miles from the beginning of Neilson Rd.) You should see a post with a sign there saying "Welcome to Bear's Den."

<u>Driving Directions from Route 2 East of New Salem</u>: In Orange take Exit 16 off Route 2 West, then take Route 202 South. Soon Route 202 South will be joined by Route 122 South. In 0.9 miles they will separate. Continue on 202 South 0.4 miles and then turn right onto Elm Street. Go 0.7 miles and then turn left onto Neilson Rd. There will be two pull-off areas on the right. Park in the second pull-off area (0.5 miles from the beginning of Neilson Rd.). You should see a post there with a sign saying "Welcome to Bear's Den."

<u>Driving Directions from Route I-91</u>: Take Exit 16 from Route I-91 in Holyoke. Then take Route 202 North and continue to New Salem. There will be two signs for entering New Salem. From the second sign (the one on the right) go 6.4 miles and then turn left onto Elm Street. Go 0.7 miles on Elm Street and then turn left onto Neilson Road. There will be two pull-off areas on the right. Park in the second area (0.5 miles from the beginning of Neilson Rd.). You should see a post there with a sign saying "Welcome to Bear's Den."

<u>What to Expect</u>: Bear's Den Reservation is owned and managed by the Trustees of Reservations. The falls are not extremely high (about 10 feet), but are picturesque because you can get quite close to them and they are divided by a rock. The falls and small pool beneath them have carved out the rocks so there are several cliffs above them.

Hunting is permitted in this area, so wear bright colors in the fall. There are no rest rooms and there is no entrance fee.

Trail Information: Follow the trail downhill toward the stream. To get to the bottom of the falls, take the main trail and look for two yellow arrows painted on trees. Turn left at these arrows to go up some rocks, dirt, and one log step. You can hear and eventually see the falls below you from the top of this area. From there it's a very short, but somewhat steep, walk down to the falls. The distance from the parking lot to the falls is about 0.1 mile.

Nearby Waterfalls and Trails with Wildflowers: Gunn Brook Falls in Sunderland; Slatestone Brook Falls in North Sunderland; High Ledges Wildlife Sanctuary in Shelburne; and Mount Sugarloaf State Reservation in South Deerfield (all in Massachusetts)

1 Campbells Falls

Campbells Falls State Park
North Norfolk, Connecticut   Litchfield County and
Southfield, Massachusetts   Berkshire County
See Connecticut

8 Cascade Falls

North Adams, Massachusetts   Berkshire County

See Picture No. 46MA.

Driving Directions from Route 8 in Pittsfield: Take Route 8 North to North Adams. When Route 2 joins Route 8 in North Adams, follow the signs for Route 2 and Route 8. When Route 2 separates from Route 8, go right on Route 2. (This will be Route 2 West towards Williamstown.) Go 1.2 miles from this turn to Marion Avenue of the left. Turn left onto Marion Avenue and drive 0.3 miles to the end of Marion Avenue. There will be a small parking area to the right of the road just before the end of Marion Avenue. It is large enough for two cars.

Driving Directions from the North or East: Follow Route 8 South or Route 2 West to North Adams until they join each other. From this junction continue on Route 2 West for 2 miles to Marion Avenue on the left. Turn left onto Marion Avenue and go 0.3 miles to the end of Marion Avenue. There will be a small parking area to the right of the road just before the end of Marion Avenue. It is large enough for two cars.

What to Expect: Cascade Falls consists of two waterfalls, each being 10 to 15 feet high. They are a little hard to get close to. I crossed the stream on rocks to get the picture in this book. However, the brook is not deep, nor rapid.

I found some Spring wildflowers along the trail in May, so I listed the flowers that were blooming and went back again in June to list what was blooming then.

This area is owned by the town of North Adams. There is no fee and there are no rest room facilities.

Trail Information: The trail to Cascade Falls begins at the end of Marion Avenue and goes straight in front of the parking area on the right side of the road. The trail is not marked, but is evident most of the way. It goes over a bridge and then continues straight.

The place where it is a little confusing is where it seems to disappear at the edge of the brook. Walk on the edge of the brook for a short way, and then the trail continues beside the brook. This trail can be muddy and slippery during rainy seasons. There are no large hills to climb, but there are a few fairly steep up and down areas. The trail crosses several tiny streams which are easy to cross over. It takes about 40 minutes to go to and from the falls if you are walking at a moderate speed without stopping.

Nearby Waterfalls and Trails with Wildflowers listed in this book: Pecks Brook Falls in Adams; Mount Greylock State Reservation (Jones Nose and CCC Dynamite Trails) in Cheshire and New Ashford; and Wahconah Falls in Dalton (all in Massachusetts)

Nearby Trails with Wildflowers listed in my book *Wildflowers of the Berkshires Where and When They Bloom Vol. 1*: Field Farm in Williamstown, Massachusetts

9 Chapelbrook Falls

Chapelbrook Reservation
South Ashfield, Massachusetts   Franklin County

See Picture No. 47MA.

Driving Directions from the North: Follow Route 112 South until it meets Route 116 in Ashfield. Then turn left onto Route 116 South. Go 2.4 miles and when Route 116 turns left continue straight onto Williamsburg Road following the sign "To South 9 Williamsburg". Go 2.2 miles and you will find a small parking area just before a bridge. That is the parking area for Chapelbrook Reservation.

<u>Driving Directions from Route I-91</u>: Take Exit 24 from Route I-91 onto Route 116 North. Go on Route 116 North about 12.8 miles through Conway and into the outskirts of Ashfield. When Route 116 North goes right, you will turn left onto Williamsburg Road following the sign "To South 9 Williamsburg". Go 2.2 miles on Williamsburg Road and you will find a small parking area just before a bridge. That is the parking area for Chapelbrook Reservation.

<u>What to Expect</u>: You can see the top of the falls from the bridge near the parking area. However, the view is much better from the bottom of the falls. Chapelbrook Falls is actually a series of three waterfalls. The first one is about 10 feet high, the second one roughly 15 feet high, and the third about 25 feet high for a total height of 50 feet.

This property, as well as several others mentioned in this book, is owned by the Trustees of Reservations. I have seen these falls in both wet and dry conditions, and they are much better during or soon after wet weather. I went to this area several times and listed the wildflowers I saw along the road into the reservation. I am including them in this book for those also interested in wildflowers. The number of flowers in this area was minimal. There are no rest rooms and there is no entrance fee.

<u>Trail Information</u>: Walk across the bridge and across the street from the parking area. Turn onto the road that goes left after the bridge. To get to the falls you will need to go left again onto a short trail.

<u>Nearby Waterfalls and Trails with Wildflowers listed in this book</u>: Mount Sugarloaf in South Deerfield; Gunn Brook Falls in Sunderland; Slatestone Brook in North Sunderland; and High Ledges in Shelburne (all in Massachusetts)

10 Gunn Brook Falls

Sunderland, Massachusetts   Franklin County

See Picture No. 48MA.

Driving Directions from the North: Take Route 63 South through Montague until you reach a junction with Route 47. Turn right onto 47 South and go for 3.4 miles where you will find Falls Road on the right. Turn right onto Falls Road and go about 1 mile where you will find a long narrow pond on the right (called Chard Pond on the map). Immediately after that, turn right onto an unmarked dirt road (Gunn Cross Road). Go 0.25 miles on this road to the top of a hill where you will find a small parking area on the right. You can hear the falls as soon as you step out of the car.

Driving Directions from the South: From the junction of Route 116 and Route 47 in Sunderland, go north on Route 47 for about 1.5 miles. Bear left onto Falls Road and go about 1 mile where you will find a long narrow pond on the right (called Chard Pond on the map). Immediately after that, turn right onto an unmarked dirt road (Gunn Cross Road).   Go 0.25 miles on this road to the top of a hill where you will find a small parking area on the right. You can hear the falls as soon as you step out of the car.

What to Expect: Gunn Brook Falls is actually two waterfalls, each about 15 feet high with a ledge between them. They are in the woods where wildflowers bloom in the Spring. When I was there it was too late to see any Spring wildflowers blooming, but I documented a few plants that were there and would have bloomed earlier. There are no rest rooms and there is no entrance fee.

Trail Information: The parking area is near the top of the falls. There is a short unmarked trail going down to the bottom of the falls. The trail is made of soil, roots, and natural rock steps. It is short and fairly steep. It could be slippery if wet,.so wear shoes or boots with treads such as hiking boots.

Nearby Waterfalls and Trails with Wildflowers listed in this book: Slatestone Brook Falls in North Sunderland; Mount Sugarloaf State Reservation in South Deerfield; High Ledges Wildlife Sanctuary in Shelburne; Chapelbrook Reservation in South Ashfield; and Bear's Den Falls in New Salem (all in Massachusetts)

11 High Ledges Wildlife Sanctuary

Shelburne, Massachusetts   Franklin County

Driving Directions from the Rotary in Greenfield: Take the exit to Route 2 West (Mohawk Trail) and follow this highway for 5.5 miles into Shelburne where you will see Little Mohawk Road on the right. Turn right off Route 2 onto this road. Go up Little Mohawk Road for 1.4 miles. Turn left onto Patten Road at the large map sign. Follow Patten Road for 1.4 miles. When Patten Road turns right, turn right. (Do not take Tower Road.) Patten Road becomes a dirt road. Follow signs for High Ledges.

After the previously mentioned 1.4 miles on Patten Road, there will be a dirt road on the left with a tiny sign for High Ledges. You will see a stone wall to the right of this road. Turn left. This road is fairly bumpy, so you will need to drive slowly. Go 0.6 miles to the parking area near a metal gate placed there to prevent the entrance of motor vehicles. This area is large enough to hold several cars. There is quite a view on the way back to Route 2.

Driving Directions from Route 2 West of Shelburne: Follow Route 2 East towards Shelburne. After the sign for Shelburne on the left side, go 4 miles and look for a spire of the First Congregational Church of Shelburne. Just past the church you will find Little Mohawk Road on the left. Turn left onto Little Mohawk Road and drive for about 1.4 miles. Turn left onto Patten Road at the large map sign. Follow Patten Road for 1.4 miles. When Patten Road turns right, turn right. (Do not take Tower Road.) Patten Road becomes a dirt road. Follow signs for High Ledges.

After the previously mentioned 1.4 miles on Patten Road, there will be a dirt road on the left with a tiny sign for High Ledges. You will see a stone wall to the right of this road. Turn left. This road is fairly bumpy, so you will need to drive slowly. Go 0.6 miles to the parking area near a metal bar designed to keep out motorized vehicles. This area is large enough to hold several cars. There is quite a view on the way back to Route 2.

What to Expect: Part of the property at High Ledges was donated to the Massachusetts Audubon Society by Elsworth (Dutch) and Mary Barnard. The Audubon Society has added to the original donated property by buying some adjacent land.

The beginning of the trail is on a dirt road. After that, the trail is made of soil, rocks, roots, and leaves. It has up and down areas which are occasionally steep. Part of the trail can be wet, muddy, and slippery during the Spring and wet weather, so wear boots with tread such as hiking boots.

The trail that I followed in High Ledges is mainly in the woods, so most of the flowers bloom in the Spring. Thus, I went to this area quite often in the Spring, but not as often after that. Sometimes in the Summer and Fall I only observed the flowers in the field near the parking lot.

In the beginning of July and the middle of September I went into the Gentian Swamp which had some unusual flowers. These are included in my wildflower lists. I have been told that this area also has Swamp Milkweed, Leatherleaf, Round-leaved Sundew, Joe-Pye Weed, Boneset [Thoroughwort], Monkey Flower and Round-leaved Ragwort which bloom at other times.

There is a portable toilet near the cabin. It is usually there from Memorial Day to Columbus Day. Since this is a wildlife sanctuary no hunting, dogs, or horses are allowed. Motorized vehicles are allowed only on the entry road. There is no entry fee.

The entry road is closed to motor vehicles during snow and mud season (approximately from Thanksgiving to early May). People can walk on it, but not drive on it at that time.

I did not see any Larger Yellow Lady's Slippers on my walks, but I have been told that they bloom around Memorial Day.

Trail Information: During most of my trips to High Ledges I took the same trails. I went past the iron gate and down the road that is closed to motorized vehicles. I saw a sign for the Lady's Slipper Trail on the right, but, except for the beginning of June, I went right past it. I never went on the West Brook Trail on the left.

After skipping the West Brook Trail, I took a left fork and then a right fork toward a cabin which often has maps. After the cabin are ledges which give an excellent view.

To follow the trail I took, continue past the ledges and you will see a sign for the Lady's Slipper Trail. Follow that trail to the right and look for the blue circles on trees which tell you that you are on a trail going away from the parking area. From then on, continue following the trail markers and be sure to stay on the Lady's Slipper Trail. Do not go on the West Brook Trail, the North Trail, or the Wolves Den Trail.

Eventually, you will find that the trail markers will be yellow. This will mean that you are going back toward the parking area. Continue following these yellow markers and you will eventually come to a road. At this road turn left to go up to the parking area and Sanctuary entry road.

Occasionally, I also went to the Gentian Swamp area which had some unusual flowers. To get to this area take the Wolves Den Trail to the left the second time it meets the Lady's Slipper Trail. Soon after that you will see another Wolves Den Trail sign. At this sign do not turn left as this sign indicates, but go straight into the Gentian Swamp which has a boardwalk. Turn around at the end of the boardwalk and go back to the Lady's Slipper Trail. Then turn left, following the yellow markers back to the road. Turn left at the road to go back up to the parking area and the Sanctuary entry road.

Nearby Waterfalls and Trails with Wildflowers listed in this book: Mount Sugarloaf State Reservation in South Deerfield; Slatestone Brook Falls in North Sunderland; Gunn Brook Falls in Sunderland; Chapelbrook Reservation in South Ashfield; and Bear's Den Falls in New Salem (all in Massachusetts).

12 Mount Greylock State Reservation

Cheshire and New Ashford, Massachusetts
Berkshire County

Driving Directions from the South: Take Route 7 North from
Pittsfield. Look for a sign for the town of Lanesboro on the
left. Go 3.3 miles from this sign and you will find a sign for
the Mount Greylock Visitors Center. This sign will point you
to a right turn onto North Main Street. Another sign says
"Wildlife Viewing Area." Follow these signs and turn right.
Go 1.8 miles, following signs to the Visitors Center. You may
want to stop at the Visitors Center which is on the right. To
get to the Jones Nose Trail from the Visitors Center, drive 3.8
miles to a parking lot on the right.

Driving Directions from the North: Take Route 7 South
towards Lanesboro. After the sign for entering Lanesboro, go
3.9 miles and look on the right for a sign "Wildlife Viewing
Area" with a left arrow. Follow this sign by turning left onto
North Main Street. Go 1.8 miles, following signs to the
Visitors Center. You may want to stop at the Visitors Center
which is on the right. To get to the Jones Nose Trail from the
Visitors Center, drive 3.8 miles to a parking lot on the right.

What to Expect: Mount Greylock is the highest mountain in
Massachusetts at 3,491 feet above sea level. Above the 2,600
foot elevation may be found the only sub alpine, boreal or
spruce-fir forest in the state. These are normally found much
further north. The top of the mountain has an observation
tower where you may see for about 70 miles on a clear day.

Bascom Lodge (413-743-1591), also at the summit, has modern rest rooms, rooms that are available for overnight stays, and a shop with books and souvenirs. Food is also available at Bascom Lodge during certain hours of the day. The lodge is open from mid-May through mid-October. The auto roads accessing the Reservation are open from mid-May through about late-October. Hiking trails are still open before and after those dates.

If you are new to the area, be sure to visit the summit as well as hiking the Jones Nose and CCC Dynamite trails. There is a fee of $2 to park in the summit lot. However, there is no fee to park in the lot near the Jones Nose Trail.

The trails that I took went through woods as well as a large field. Much of it was uphill, but there were some flat areas also. The Jones Nose Trail is fairly steep in places and can be muddy and slippery, so wear hiking boots. The CCC Dynamite Trail is fairly level, and may be also accessed by a trailhead at the intersections of the Rockwell and Sperry Roads for a more moderate hike.

The wooded areas of the Jones Nose Trail and CCC Dynamite Trail have quite a few wildflowers in the Spring and the meadow area of the Jones Nose Trail has many flowers in the Summer. Because of the higher altitude of Mount Greylock compared to the surrounding region, flowers that normally bloom in the Spring down in the valleys will bloom much later on the mountain slopes. Ecologists have compared the unique transition in forest zones (Northern hardwood to Spruce-fir) from the base to the summit of Mount Greylock to walking from Pennsylvania to Maine in one day.

The Visitor Center (413-499-4262) is on Rockwell Road and is mentioned in the Driving Directions. It is open from 9AM to 4PM daily, year-round. It has information, trail maps, exhibits and rest rooms and is a good place to get oriented if you're unfamiliar with the area.

Hunting is allowed at Mount Greylock, so wear bright colors in the Fall (generally from mid-October to mid-December) and stay on marked trails. Note that hunting is not permitted in Massachusetts on Sundays. For additional information on Mount Greylock State Reservation visit www.massparks.org on the internet.

Trail Information There are several signs at the edge of the parking lot. Follow the sign for the Jones Nose Trail. The trail will go through a narrow band of trees and shrubs and then enter a huge field. The trail is well-worn so it will be obvious. It goes uphill, then slightly downhill, then uphill again, but is not very steep.

Then the trail goes into the woods. Again, the trail is evident. There are steep places on this part of the trail as well as sections that are not so steep and are fairly level.

Eventually you will come to a fork in the trail. There will be a sign that says "CCC Dynamite Trail" pointing to the left. Go left. The terrain on this trail is fairly level. I continued until I came to a tiny brook with a stone to cross it and a small waterfall over a rock to the right of the trail. This waterfall is obvious in wet weather, but is harder to notice when it is dry. At that point I turned around. The trail, however, continued further.

Nearby Waterfalls and Trails with Wildflowers listed in this book: Pecks Brook Falls in Adams; Cascade Falls in North Adams; and Wahconah Falls in Dalton (all in Massachusetts)

Nearby Trails with Wildflowers listed in my books *Wildflowers of the Berkshires Where and When They Bloom Vol. 1 and Vol. 2*: Field Farm in Williamstown and Springside Park in Pittsfield (Vol. 1); also trails across from Hancock Shaker Village in Hancock; Canoe Meadows in Pittsfield; and Arrowhead in Pittsfield (Vol. 2). All are in Massachusetts.

13 *Mount Sugarloaf State Reservation*

South Deerfield, Massachusetts   Franklin County

Driving Directions from I-91 North: Take Exit 24 (South Deerfield.) Go left on Routes 5 and 10 North over I-91 to meet Route 116. Go 1.1 miles on Route 116 South to an intersection of Route 116 and Sugarloaf Street. The main entrance to Mount Sugarloaf is just to the left of this intersection. Turn left, pass the entrance, and turn right into the parking area. The trail starts from this parking area.

What to Expect: Mount Sugarloaf is accessible by car and by foot. There is a paved road to the right of the lower parking area that goes up to the top of the mountain. You can get a great view of the surrounding area from the summit. There are also picnic tables and modern rest rooms up there. You might want to go there and enjoy the view before or after your hike.

The road to the top is not open in the early Spring. It usually opens around Mother's Day and closes around Columbus Day. There is a fee of $2 for parking in the upper parking lot on weekends and holidays. This is subject to change. There is no fee for the lower parking lot.

There are many Flowering Dogwood trees which seem to grow wild along the trail from the lower parking lot. They look lovely when they bloom in May.

Trail Information: The trail that I took starts at the lower parking lot by Sugarloaf Street. The trail initially is in the woods. Then it goes left under some power lines into an open area. After that, the rest of the trail is in the woods. There are some red blazes to mark the trail. Soon after entering the woods, the trail goes uphill. There is a fork in the trail, but these trails eventually meet. Sometimes I took the left fork and sometimes the right.

Part way up the trail there is a sign pointing to the summit. Follow this sign. Soon after this point, the trail becomes quite steep for a short distance and goes up to the road. When you get to the road, you can continue to the summit or walk down the road. I walked down the road and often found some very nice, and sometimes unusual, wildflowers on the left side of the road growing in the ledges. This road goes back down and leads to the entrance to Mount Sugarloaf just beside the parking lot.

Nearby Waterfalls and Trails with Wildflowers listed in this book: Gunn Brook Falls in Sunderland; Slatestone Brook Falls in North Sunderland; High Ledges Wildlife Sanctuary in Shelburne; Chapelbrook Falls in South Ashfield; and Bear's Den Falls in New Salem (all in Massachusetts).

14 The Norcross Wildlife Sanctuary at Tupper Hill

Monson and Wales, Massachusetts   Hampden County

Driving Directions from the Massachusetts Turnpike (I-90): Get off I-90 at Exit 8 (Palmer). Turn right onto Route 32 South. Route 32 South turns left at 0.6 miles in Palmer. From that point continue on Route 32 South 6.0 miles and then look for Wales Road on the left. In addition to the street sign, there will be a sign on the left saying "To Rte 19 Wales". Turn left onto Wales Rd. The road will split at 0.4 miles. Stay right at that split and follow Wales Road an additional 3.2 miles to turn right onto Peck Rd. The entrance to "Tupper Hill, The Norcross Wildlife Sanctuary" is 0.1 miles on the left down Peck Road.

What to Expect: Norcross Wildlife Sanctuary is different from most of the other places covered in this book because it has a combination of wildflowers that have been planted and wildflowers that were originally in the area. Many of the planted flowers are in groups and have both common and scientific names on labels close to them.

This sanctuary was established by Arthur D. Norcross and is maintained by the Norcross Wildlife Foundation, Inc. Plants grown in this area are native to the eastern seaboard from Canada to the Carolinas.

Norcross Wildlife Sanctuary has a Visitors Center and picnic tables just past a large parking lot. In the Visitors Center there are trail maps available as well as information about the various habitats at Norcross and some of the plants that grow in each one.

Norcross also has two natural history museums. One is in the Visitors Center. The exhibits in these museums provide information about animals, plants, insects, and minerals of the northeast. A naturalist provides educational programs.

There are 2 miles of marked walking trails. Many of them are covered with wood chips and are soft to walk on. They are also quite flat. I went on some, but not all, of these trails. The trails are open from mid-April through November if trail conditions permit it.

No pets are allowed. There is no fee, but guests must register in the Visitors Center.

Norcross is open to the public from 9 AM to 4 PM. From June through October they are open every day except Sundays, legal holidays, and Saturdays before a legal holidays that fall on a Monday. From November to June they are closed on Mondays as well as the days already mentioned.

For further information call 413-267-9654 or find their website at www.norcrossws.org.

Trail Information: There are many trails and areas with wildflowers at Norcross. I soon found that some areas had more wildflowers than others. Based on this information, I followed certain trails to specific areas on a fairly consistent basis. My readers can follow the trails that I took or look at my wildflower lists and decide where they would like to go. Norcross has a Sanctuary Trail Map that will be helpful, especially to those who want to choose their own course. I will give directions based on my walks.

There are two doors from the Visitors Center that go out to the trails. Take the one on the left (past the rest rooms). From there go down the sidewalk. Turn right, walk for a short distance, and turn left at a sign for the Short Trail. The path to the Short Trail is called the Hickory Grove on the map.

At the end of the trail through the Hickory Grove is the Short Trail, which is a fenced-in area with many wildflowers and several paths. There are gates at two places where visitors can enter and exit. Go in the gate from the Hickory Grove, walk along the various paths of the Short Trail, and then go out the other gate.

After that, go across the street to continue on a path into the Conifer Grove. This will be in the opposite direction as the arrow in the trail sign. Walk past the Acid Rock Garden, skip the Upland Shrub area, and turn right. Continue walking and when you come to a fork, take a slight left, following a sign that says to "Boardwalk, Lime Cobbles, and Pine Barren Garden." (This is the Lower Trail on the map.)

Go right onto the Boardwalk and right again at the Pond Trail. This will bring you up to the Coastal Kettle Pond. Follow the trail around the pond, initially going right. After going around the pond, turn right to leave the pond area. Go down the boardwalk, turn right toward the Circle Garden, and then turn right into the Circle Garden. After checking out the flowers in the Circle Garden, go left into the Lime Flower Cobbles.

After seeing the flowers in the Lime Flower Cobbles, go up the steps to the field. Turn left to walk near the edge of the field, then turn right to continue around the edge of the field. When you see the sign for the Pine Barren Garden, turn left to enter the garden.

After that, return to the Visitor Center. Skip the Holly Grove and go straight towards and onto the Lower Trail. Turn left at the sign on the right for the "Boardwalk, Lime Cobbles, and Pine Barren Garden".

There were a few times that I varied my walk, so I am also giving directions with my lists of flowers.

15 Pecks Brook Falls

Adams, Massachusetts   Berkshire County

See Picture Nos. 49MA and 50MA.

<u>Driving Directions from North Adams</u>: Take Route 8 South from North Adams toward Adams. Look on the right for the sign for entering Adams. From that sign go 1.4 miles and then turn right onto Friend Street. There will be several jogs, but continue on this road 1.7 miles. Then turn right onto West Mountain Road. Go 0.1 miles and you will see high tension wires. Go another 0.1 miles and you will see orange and white gas pipelines on both sides of the road. There is no parking area as such, but there are several areas on the right side of the road wide enough to park a car.

<u>Driving Directions from Route 8   south of Adams</u>: Take Route 8 North into Cheshire. From the sign on the right for Cheshire continue 5.7 miles on Route 8 North. Then look to your left for Fred Mason Road. Turn left and go on Fred Mason Road for 0.9 miles. Then continue straight. This road is called West Road on the map, but there seems to be no road sign verifying this. Go on West Road for 2.2 miles, then turn left onto West Mountain Road. Follow West Mountain Road 0.1 miles and you will see high tension wires. Go another 0.1

miles and you will see orange and white gas pipelines on both sides of the road. There is no parking area as such, but there are several areas on the right side of the road wide enough to park a car.

What to Expect: Pecks Brook has three separated areas of falls. The top two falls can be seen at the same time, but the lower falls can be seen only by itself.

The top waterfall drops about 20-30 feet. It is actually a series of several falls, one being fairly high. However, much of this waterfall cannot be seen as it is behind rock. The middle waterfall is broken up also. It has a total drop of 12 to15 feet. The lower waterfall is two falls. The upper part is 12 to 15 feet high and the lower part is about 6 feet.high.

The area is woodland. I listed the flowers blooming along the trails.

There are no rest rooms. but the area is not far from the town of Adams.

Trail Information: There are two unmarked entrances to the trail which leads to the waterfalls. These entrances are just past (up the road from) the right hand gas pipeline. Take one of these entrances and almost immediately you will find a trail. Turn right and go down the trail. The trail is fairly steep at first. It is marked with one white marker on a tree. You can hear the falls from the trail.

There are waterfalls at three different places. The trail goes above all three waterfalls. You can see the top and middle falls from the trail, but if you go to the left slightly off the trail you can see them better. They are somewhat in back of you as you go down the trail.

Continue down the trail a little farther to find the lower waterfall. You will have to go off the trail and to the left onto a smaller path that goes down to the brook to see this falls. This path is somewhat steep. You can make your way back up the stream bed for a closer look at the lower falls. There are fallen trees in various places. To get a good picture of the lower falls, I took off my footwear and walked across the brook.

The trail to see the top and middle falls is less than 0.1 mile. You can see the lower waterfalls in another 0.1 mile or less.

Nearby Waterfalls and Trails with Wildflowers listed in this book: Cascade Falls in North Adams; Mount Greylock State Reservation (Jones Nose and CCC Dynamite Trails) in Cheshire and New Ashford; and Wahconah Falls in Dalton. (all in Massachusetts).

Nearby Trails with Wildflowers listed in my books *Wildflowers of the Berkshires   Where and When They Bloom Vol. 1 and Vol. 2*: Field Farm in Williamstown, and Springside Park in Pittsfield (Vol. 1); also the trails across from Hancock Shaker Village in Hancock, Canoe Meadows and Arrowhead in Pittsfield, and Pleasant Valley in Lenox (Vol. 2). All are in Massachusetts.

16 Sanderson Brook Falls

Chester-Blandford State Forest
Chester and Blandford, Massachusetts   Hampden County

See Picture No. 51MA.

<u>Driving Directions from the East</u>: Follow Route 20 West through Huntington. You will see a sign "Entering Town of Chester." From that sign drive 2.4 miles and look for a small bridge and two signs - one saying "Sanderson Brook Road" and a larger one saying "Sanderson Brook Falls." Turn left onto Sanderson Brook Road. There is a parking lot to the right.

<u>Driving Directions from Route 20 in Lee</u>: Take Route 20 East out of Lee. Route 8 North will join 20 East and then later they will separate. Continue on Route 20 East past that separation point for 2.8 miles, and then look to the right for a sign for Chester. From that sign drive 4.1 miles and look for two signs - one saying "Sanderson Brook Road" and a larger one saying "Sanderson Brook Falls." Turn right into Sanderson Brook Road. There is a parking lot to the right.

<u>What to Expect</u>: Sanderson Brook Falls is actually a series of falls and cascades. The total drop is about 70 feet. There are many rocks and boulders in the area. There are also several tree trunks that have fallen into the waterfall area.

Because most of the trail is a road, there is enough light for many Spring wildflowers. Therefore, I went to this area four times in order to record the wildflowers that were blooming at different times. I made lists of the flowers to include in this book for people who are interested in wildflowers as well as waterfalls.

There are often maps of the area near the parking lot. There are no rest rooms and there is no entry fee.

Trail Information: To get to Sanderson Brook Falls, walk up Sanderson Brook Road. There is a metal bar to keep motor vehicles out, so you will have to climb over or duck under it. The road eventually goes slightly uphill, but it is a fairly easy walk. The road has three metal grate bridges which go over Sanderson Brook.

After crossing the third bridge, look for a blue arrow on a tree to the right of the road. This arrow points to the right to a fairly narrow trail which goes downhill and soon leads to the falls.

The road and trail to the falls take about 60 minutes round trip if walking at a moderate pace without stopping.

Nearby Trail with Wildflowers listed in my book *Wildflowers of the Berkshires   Where and When They Bloom   Vol. 1*: Tyringham Cobble in Tyringham, Massachusetts

17 Slatestone Brook Falls

Sunderland, Massachusetts   Franklin County

See Picture No. 52MA.

Driving Directions from the South: From the junction of Routes 116 and 47 in Sunderland, go north on Route 47 for about 1.4 miles and bear left onto Falls Road. In about 1.6 miles you will find a low-sided stone bridge over the Slatestone Brook. The falls are just to the right of the bridge. There is no parking area, but since there isn't much traffic you can stop on either side of the bridge. The area before the bridge has a little room to pull off.

Driving Directions from the North: Take Route 63 South through Montague until you reach a junction with Route 47. Turn right onto Route 47 South and go 3.4 miles where you will find Falls Road on the right. Go right onto Falls Road and in about 1.6 miles you will find a low-sided stone bridge over the Slatestone Brook. The falls are just to the right of the bridge. There is no parking area, but since there isn't much traffic you can stop on either side of the bridge. The area before the bridge has a little room to pull off.

What to Expect: Slatestone Brook Falls is actually a series of cascades. In all, it drops 35 to 40 feet. The falls were quite impressive shortly after rain had fallen in late June and early August. However, the amount of water may diminish during dry weather. After the falls, the brook runs under the road and into the Connecticut River.   There were some wildflowers in the area on both sides of the road, so I listed them during both visits. There is no entry fee and there are no rest rooms.

Trail Information: Since this waterfall is beside the road, there is no trail.

Nearby Waterfalls and Trails with Wildflowers listed in this book: Gunn Brook Falls in Sunderland; Mount Sugarloaf State Reservation in South Deerfield; High Ledges Wildlife Sanctuary in Shelburne; Chapelbrook Reservation in South Ashfield; and Bear's Den Falls in New Salem (all in Massachusetts).

18 Wahconah Falls

Wahconah Falls State Park
Dalton, Massachusetts   Berkshire County

See Picture No. 53MA.

Driving Directions from the North, South, or West: Follow
Route 7 and/or 20 into Pittsfield. Then follow Route 9 East
toward Dalton. Route 9 East will be joined by Route 8 South.
Continue into Dalton on Route 9 East and 8 South. In Dalton
9 East and 8 South will separate. Follow 9 East and 8A North
to the left.

From that intersection go about 2.3 miles and you will see a
sign on the right "Wahconah Falls State Park" with an arrow
to the right. Follow that sign and turn right onto North Street.
Continue straight onto Wahconah Falls Road which becomes
unpaved. A large parking lot for the park and the falls is on
the right about 0.4 miles from the beginning of North Street.
The sign for the park is on the right also.

Driving Directions from the East: Take Route 9 West and 8A
South toward Dalton. Look for the sign saying "Entering
Dalton" on the left. From that sign go 0.4 miles and you will
see a sign on the right "Wahconah Falls State Park" with an
arrow to the left. Go 0.1 mile and turn left onto North Street.
Continue straight onto Wahconah Falls Road which becomes
a dirt road. A large parking lot for the park and the falls is on
the right about 0.4 miles from the beginning of North Street.
The sign for the park is on the right also.

What to Expect: Wahconah Falls is about 40 feet high and is
often as wide as it is high. The trail to the falls is about 0.1
miles and is not steep. You can see some of the falls without
going down near the water. If you decide to go down next to

the water, however, you will have to go down a fairly steep bank. The falls are fuller during a rainy season, but they also look fairly good if it has not rained lately.

There are more trails than the one to the falls in this park. There are also picnic tables, metal containers for a fire, and a self-composting toilet. There is no entrance fee. This park is open to hunting during statewide hunting seasons, so wear bright clothing in the fall.

Trail Information: From the far end of the parking lot you will see a bar to prevent motor vehicles from going down the trail. Walk past that bar and go downhill to your right. Continue downhill about 0.1 mile to reach the falls.

Nearby Waterfall listed in this book: Pecks Brook Falls in Adams, Massachusetts

Nearby Trails with Wildflowers listed in my books *Wildflowers of the Berkshires Where and When They Bloom Vol. 1 and Vol. 2*: Springside Park in Pittsfield (Vol. 1); also Arrowhead, and Canoe Meadows in Pittsfield, trails across from Hancock Shaker Village in Hancock, and Pleasant Valley in Lenox (Vol. 2). All are in Massachusetts.

New York

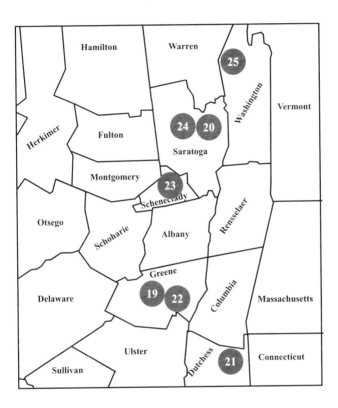

19. Ashley Falls - Haines Falls, NY
20. Bog Meadow Nature Trail - Saratoga Springs, NY
21. Harlem Valley Rail Trail - Millerton, NY
22. Kaaterskill Falls - Haines Falls/Palenville, NY
23. Plotter Kill Falls - Rotterdam, NY
24. Railroad Run - Saratoga Springs, NY
25. Shelving Rock Falls - Fort Ann, NY

19 Ashley Falls

North-South Lake area of the Catskill Forest Preserve
Haines Falls, New York   Greene County

See Picture No. 54NY.

<u>Driving Directions</u>: Follow directions for Kaaterskill Falls. From the parking area for Kaaterskill Falls drive about 1.3 miles and turn right onto North Lake Road (Green County Route 18). Be sure to bear right at the first intersection to stay on that road. From the turn onto North Lake Road, drive about 2.2 miles to find a sign which says "North - South Lake Public Campground and Day Use Area." At the first fork in the road after the registration booth bear left. Shortly after that you will come to a stop sign. Bear left again following the sign to "North Lake Picnic & Beach Area ... Mary's Glen Trail." Go approximately 0.4 miles more and you will find a parking area on the left.

<u>What to Expect</u>: Ashley Falls is quite lovely in the spring or when there has been quite a bit of rainfall. It is within the North - South Lake area of the Catskill Forest Preserve and is run by the New York State Department of Environmental Conservation.   The area contains many hiking trails, campgrounds, picnic areas, rest rooms, and a beach.

The area is open from May to October 28. There is a fee of $6 per car for day use of the area. Seniors (62+) are allowed in free from Monday through Friday.

For further information or to reserve a campsite call 518-589-5058 or 1-800-456-2267, or go to the website *www.reserveamerica.com.*

Mary's Glen Trail leads to the trail for Ashley Falls after a short walk. The trail is fairly flat, but it is rocky in places. Other places are muddy or wet depending on the amount of rain that has fallen recently.

To get the best perspective of the falls, you have to walk into the brook. This can be done on dry rocks if the weather has been dry. However, if you want to see the falls at their best, go during or after wet weather. You can still walk on rocks, but some of them may be somewhat under water. Wear boots in wet weather.

Trail Information: Mary's Glen Trail begins just before the parking area on the same side of the road.   Follow the red markers on Mary's Glen Trail for about 0.2 miles. You will see two signs - one saying "Trail" and the other saying "Trail to Ashley Falls" Follow the "Trail to Ashley Falls" sign to the right for a very short distance.

Nearby Waterfalls listed in this book: Kaaterskill Falls and Bastion Falls in Haines Falls and Palenville, New York

20 Bog Meadow Brook Nature Trail

Saratoga Springs, New York   Saratoga County

Driving Directions from the South: Follow the Northway (Route I-87 North) to Exit 14. Go right at 9P North. Follow signs to Route 29. Turn right on Henning Road which also says "to 29" (first stop light). Go 0.9 miles to the next stop light and go right onto Route 29 East. Go past another stop light and look for Gilbert Street. Do not turn, but continue straight for 0.4 miles and look to the right for a short loop entry with a sign "Bog Meadow Brook Nature Trail."

<u>Driving Directions from the North</u>: Follow the Northway (Route I-87 South) toward Saratoga Springs. Get off at Exit 15 onto Route 50 North. Follow arrows to Route 29 East. (not Truck Route East 29.) After 1 mile, turn left onto Route 29 East. Bog Meadow Brook Nature Trail will be 0.5 miles on the right.

<u>What to Expect</u>: Because there was water on both sides of the trail, the sun was able to reach the area near the trail in most places at least part of the day. Therefore, there were wildflowers blooming beside the trail from Spring through Fall.

This trail is quite flat.   During wet weather there is one place on the trail that gets quite wet, so rubber boots or hiking boots are recommended.

There is no fee and there are no rest rooms. However, there are various stores nearby. Pets are allowed, but they are to be on a leash and you are to clean up after them. Stay on the trail and watch out for Poison Ivy and ticks.

<u>Trail Information</u>: The trail at Bog Meadow Brook is built on former railroad tracks. The entrance to the trail is right off the parking area. The present trail area was built up for railroad tracks and has water on both sides. The tracks are gone and the railroad ties are gone from the beginning of the trail, but further on (after about ½ to ¾ of a mile) the ties are still part of the trail.

There is a bridge part way up the trail. Water flows from one side to the other underneath the bridge. There are several signs with information about the trail and wetland habitats. This trail is a Saratoga Springs Open Space project. There are markers on trees every ¼ mile. I usually hiked up to the 1 mile marker which is on a tree to the right of the trail. Hiking up to this marker and back should take about 1 hour if walked at a moderate speed without stopping.

Nearby Waterfalls and Trails with Wildflowers listed in this book: Railroad Run in Saratoga Springs; Shelving Rock Falls in Fort Ann (both in New York); and D&H Rail Trail in Rupert, Vermont.

21 Harlem Valley Rail Trail

Millerton, New York   Dutchess County

Driving Directions from the South: Take Route 22 North into Millerton. Route 44 East will join Route 22 North. Continue on Route 22 North and 44 East. When these two routes separate, turn right and follow Route 44 East. Go less than half a block on Route 44 East and you will see a sign "Rail Trail" with an arrow pointing right. Park somewhere along the street or on South Center Street.

Driving Directions from the North: Take Route 22 South past Copake into Millerton. Turn left in Millerton when Route 44 East goes left. Within less than half a block, you will see a sign "Rail Trail" with an arrow pointing to the right. Park somewhere along the street or on South Center Street.

What to Expect: There is no entry fee. Near the beginning of the trail is a bulletin board with information about the Harlem Valley Rail Trail as well as rules for the Millerton section of the trail. Pets should be leashed. The trail is opened from dawn to dusk. There is an outdoor chemical toilet near the beginning of the trail. I saw only a few mosquitoes (none in September.)

The trail is quite flat and has a combination of sunny and shady areas. This produces a variety of wildflowers. Besides wildflowers, I also listed garden perennials that were blooming near the trail.

<u>Trail Information</u>: The Harlem Valley Rail Trail in Millerton is part of a rail trail that extends for many miles. I walked on several other areas of this trail and found the one in Millerton to be the best area for wildflowers.

The trail is made of blacktop and is about 8 feet wide. It has three bridges that cross a river that meanders back and forth. The river and the wildflowers create a pleasant view from the trail.

Part of the trail passes between two tall cliffs of rocks which were cut into for the railroad tracks. It is quite cool and damp in this area, which is especially nice on a hot summer day. Besides these attractions, there is a small farm with various farm animals that can be seen from the trail.

The trail crosses one road which is not very busy. Bicycle riders travel this trail as well as hikers.

I turned around just after the area with farm animals at a building with a greenhouse attached to it. The hike takes about 50 minutes round trip if you hike to the greenhouse and back at a medium speed without stopping.

<u>Nearby Waterfalls and Trails with Wildflowers listed in this book</u>: Kent Falls in Kent, Pine Swamp Brook Falls in Sharon, and Dean's Ravine Falls in Canaan (all in Connecticut); also Bash Bish Falls in Massachusetts.

22 Kaaterskill Falls

Catskill Forest Preserve
Haines Falls and Palenville, New York   Greene County

See Picture No. 55NY.

<u>Driving Directions from Rip Van Winkle Bridge which
crosses the Hudson River on Route 32 West from Columbia
County into Catskill, New York</u>: After crossing the Rip Van
Winkle Bridge, turn left onto Route 385 South. Continue on
this highway through Catskill. When Route 385 ends at 9W
South, take 9W South for 0.6 miles. At the junction with 23A
go straight onto 23A West. Continue on 23A all the way to
Kaaterskill Falls. Kaaterskill Creek goes under highway 23A.
You will go through Palenville and over the Kaaterskill Creek,
which is marked by a sign. The trail to Kaaterskill Falls is
about 2.5 miles past the Kaaterskill Creek sign.

There is a waterfall below Kaaterskill Falls. It is called
Bastion Falls and can be seen to the right of highway 23A.
There is a sign near Bastion Falls for Kaaterskill Falls. After
this sign, continue on the highway 0.2 miles to a parking lot
on the left.

<u>Driving Directions from the North</u>: Take the New York State
Thruway (I-87) to Exit 21 at Catskill. Go left onto Route 23
East to Route 9W South. Follow Route 9W through Catskill
to Route 23A West.   Continue on 23A all the way to
Kaaterskill Falls. Kaaterskill Creek goes under highway 23A.
You will go through Palenville and over the Kaaterskill Creek,
which is marked by a sign. The trail to Kaaterskill Falls is
about 2.5 miles past the Kaaterskill Creek sign.

There is a falls below Kaaterskill Falls. It is called Bastion
Falls and can be seen to the right of Highway 23A.

There is a sign near Bastion Falls for Kaaterskill Falls. After this sign, continue on the highway 0.2 miles to a parking lot on the left.

<u>Driving Directions from the South</u>: Take the New York State Thruway (I-87) north to Exit 20 at Saugerties. Follow Route 32 north for about 6 miles to 32A to 23A West. Continue on 23A all the way to Kaaterskill Falls. Kaaterskill Creek goes under highway 23A. You will go through Palenville and over the Kaaterskill Creek, which is marked by a sign. The trail to Kaaterskill Falls is about 2.5 miles past the sign for Kaaterskill Creek.

There is a falls below Kaaterskill Falls. It is called Bastion Falls and can be seen to the right of Highway 23A. There is a sign for Kaaterskill Falls near Bastion Falls on the right. After this sign, continue on the highway 0.2 miles to a parking lot on the left.

<u>What to Expect</u>: There are two major waterfalls in this area with cascades at various places in between these falls. The lower falls (called Bastion Falls) can be seen from Route 23A. Kaaterskill Falls is much higher and can be seen only by walking up an 0.7 mile trail. Both waterfalls are on Lake Creek.

Kaaterskill Falls is approximately 260 feet high and is the highest falls in New York State. It consists of two tiers. The upper falls drop 175 feet and the lower falls drop 85 feet. There is a list of State Land General Rules and Regulations on a bulletin board near the bottom of the trail. Kaaterskill Falls is in the Catskill Forest Preserve and is run by the New York State Department of Environmental Conservation. There are no rest rooms and there is no entry fee.

Trail Information: To get to Bastion Falls and the trail to Kaaterskill Falls from the parking lot, walk downhill on the left side of Route 23A which has a narrow shoulder for walking. Take care to stay on the shoulder since the roadway is often busy.

After you cross the bridge, you can see both Bastion Falls and the beginning of the trail to Kaaterskill Falls.

The trail to Kaaterskill Falls is quite a steep climb.   The beginning of the trail is made of rock and wood steps. Then it levels off somewhat. After that is goes up again. The trail is marked by yellow circular markers nailed to trees. You can see Lake Creek with its many cascades much of the time from the trail.

This trail is 0.7 miles one way and the ascent is 340 feet. The time to reach the peak will depend on the individual's endurance. It takes about 25 minutes to go back down at a medium speed without stopping.

Nearby Waterfall listed in this book: Ashley Falls in Haines Falls, New York.

23 Plotter Kill Falls

Plotter Kill Nature and Historic Preserve
Rotterdam, New York   Schenectady County

See Picture No. 56NY.

Driving Directions from I-90 South of Rotterdam: Take I-90 to Exit 25A to Route I-88. On Route I-88 take Exit 25 almost immediately. It is about 26.1 miles from the toll booth on Route I-90 to the Plotter Kill parking lot.

Follow the arrow left toward Route 7 and then go left onto Route 7 East. Go 0.9 miles on Route 7 East and then turn left onto Route 337 (Burdeck Street.) Go 0.6 miles on 337, then turn left onto Route 159 (Mariaville Road.) Go 23.9 miles and look to the right for a sign for the Plotter Kill parking lot.

What to Expect: There are three falls in the Plotter Kill Nature and Historical Preserve. The first two are on the Plotter Kill ("kill" meaning stream, channel, or creek). The third is in a tributary to the Plotter Kill.

Since the Plotter Kill tends to have very little water in dry weather, go in Spring or wet weather to see the falls at their best.

The trails are fairly well marked and in wet weather the falls are beautiful. However, it is difficult and also dangerous to get to the base to see them.

There are no rest rooms and there is no fee. The area is open from dawn to dusk.

Trail Information: Marked trails lead you to the top of the second and third falls. There is an unmarked trail to the right of the marked trail which goes to the top of the first falls, but there is a line across it indicating that it is considered a dangerous area since the cliff edge may be undercut.

The best way to see the top of the second and third falls is to take the Red trail most of the way. The Red trail has red marks on the trees usually circled with white.

The trail starts to the left of the bulletin board in the parking lot and begins on a boardwalk. It turns left almost immediately at a fork and then goes slightly downhill to the Plotter Kill. The trail here is muddy during wet weather.

Continue on the Red trail down steps with a railing. Go right at the bottom of the steps, then down more steps with no railing. Then cross a bridge over the Plotter Kill. After the bridge, follow the Red trail to the left. At an intersection, be sure to bear right at the red arrow.

You will soon arrive near the top of the first waterfall. There you will see the dangerous side trail mentioned before. Continue on the Red trail for less than 10 minutes and you will reach another intersection.

Look to the right and you will see a small sign with a yellow arrow saying "stream and falls." This yellow trail is a fairly steep descent at times and leads to the Plotter Kill. After you go down this trail you will see a cascade to your right. Walking to the left (downstream) will lead you to the top of the second falls. Don't get too close as the trees and dirt may give way. Go back the way you came to the Red trail and continue to the right on this trail.

After about 10 more minutes of walking on the Red trail, you will reach the top of the third waterfall. This waterfall has a cliff on one side and a very steep area on the other side.

You can go back at this point as you have seen all three waterfalls.

There are flat areas on the Red trail as well as many up and down areas. It takes about 30 minutes to walk from the parking lot to the top of the third falls taking the Red trail and walking at a moderate pace without stopping (a little longer if the yellow trail is included.). This is about a one hour round trip.

24 Railroad Run

Saratoga Springs, New York   Saratoga County

<u>Driving Directions from the Northway (Route I-87) coming from the South</u>: Take the Northway (Route I-87) to Exit 14. Go right at 9P North. Go on 9P North 1.7 miles from the end of the exit and then turn left at Circular Avenue. Go one block, bear right at the fork just past the stop sign, and continue one block more. Cross Broadway and go straight (not onto Route 50). You are now on West Circular.

Go several blocks. Pass Aletta Street on the left and immediately look for the Palmetto Fruit Company building also on the left. The Railroad Run Trail begins just past this building on West Circular.

<u>Driving Directions from the Northway (Route I-87) coming from the North</u>; Take the Northway (Route I-87 South). Get off at Exit 15 and take Route 50 South. Route 9 South and Route 29 West will join Route 50 South. Stay on Route 50 South for 2.2 miles. When Route 50 goes right, West Circular goes sharply to the right. Take the sharp right onto West Circular.

Go 0.2 miles to Aletta Street on the left and immediately look for the Palmetto Fruit Company building, also on the left. The Railroad Run Trail begins just past this building on West Circular.

<u>What to Expect</u>:   There is a sign at the beginning of the Railroad Run Trail giving its history and sponsorship.   The area was originally a segment of the D&H Railway tracks. This trail is sponsored by the Saratoga Springs Open Space Project.

There is an active group that is involved with the beauty of the Railroad Run area.   They planted more bulbs and wildflowers shortly after I finished my walks.   Therefore, there may be more flowers than I have listed.

There are no fees, mosquitoes, or rest rooms. However, this area is within a few blocks of the center of Saratoga Springs which has a visitors center, stores, and fast food restaurants.

<u>Trail Information</u>:   The Railroad Run Trail consists of two walkways approximately 8 feet wide with a raised median strip about 10 feet wide between them.   The median strip has a combination of grass, wildflowers, and plants from bulbs. Many of the wildflowers and bulbs have been planted.   There are also some garden perennials that can be seen from the trail which I also listed.

The trail on the right side of the median strip is blacktop. The one to the left of the strip consists of tiny stones similar to those found on a tennis court.   The Railroad Run Trail is traveled by people on bicycles, as well as hikers, joggers, and people walking their dogs.

I always started walking the trail on the right side of the median strip and listed flowers on that side.   I went one long block to the next road (Route 50) and then turned around and came back on the other side, usually listing only flowers I had not seen on the first side.

The walk up one side of the Railroad Run Trail and back the other side should take about 30 minutes round trip if you walk at a medium speed without stopping.

Nearby Waterfalls and Trails with Wildflowers listed in this book: Bog Meadow Nature Trail in Saratoga Springs; Shelving Rock Falls in Fort Ann (both in New York); and D&H Rail Trail in Rupert, Vermont.

25 *Shelving Rock Falls*

Lake George Trail System
Fort Ann, New York   Washington County

See Picture No. 57NY.

Driving Directions: From Route I-87 (Northway) take Exit 20 near Glens Falls. Then turn left onto New York State Route 149 East. Go 6.5 miles, then turn left onto Buttermilk Falls Road. The distance from this corner to the parking area near the falls is 12.4 miles.

The route from Buttermilk Falls Road to the parking areas near Shelving Rock Falls involves no turns, but several name changes. Go on Buttermilk Falls Road for about 3.2 miles where you will pass Twiss Road and then see Woods Road on the right. Continue straight. This road is now called Sly Pond Road. Sly Pond Road soon becomes unpaved with occasional black-top areas. After 5.9 miles Hogtown Road will come in from the right. Continue straight again and you will be on Shelving Rock Road. Continue on this road for 0.8 miles and you will see a parking lot and a sign "Lake George Trail System." It is 2.4 miles from this sign to the parking lot near the trail to the falls.

Continue on Shelving Rock Road which becomes somewhat narrow with a steep downhill grade. You will cross two brooks. The second one is Shelving Rock Brook. Shelving Rock Falls is on this brook. The bridge over Shelving Rock Brook has metal guard rails and also wooden material for fencing. There are several parking lots on the left past Shelving Rock Brook. The first parking lot past the bridge is closest to the falls.

What to Expect: There is camping near the parking lot to the left past Shelving Rock Brook. If that lot is full, there are several others beyond it. There is an outhouse in the camping area quite a ways back into the camping area and to the left. There is no entrance fee.

The picture of the falls in this book was taken during a dry period. The falls will look fuller in the Spring or shortly after a heavy rain.

Trail Information and Directions: To get to the falls, exit the parking lot and walk on the road back to Shelving Rock Brook. Cross the bridge and turn right onto an unmarked trail on the left side of the brook. The trail follows the brook downstream. There are quite a few rocks at the beginning of this trail; then it becomes dirt and leaves. Within about 10 minutes you will come to the top of the falls.

If, when you are trying to get to the bottom of the falls, you come to a place which is extremely steep, back up and try an alternate route that is not so steep. There is a safer trail that zigzags to the bottom of the falls.

Nearby Waterfalls and Trails with Wildflowers listed in this book: Railroad Run and Bog Meadow Nature Trail (both in Saratoga Springs, New York); also Moss Glen Falls in Granville; Texas Falls in Hancock: and D&H Rail Trail in Rupert (all in Vermont).

Vermont

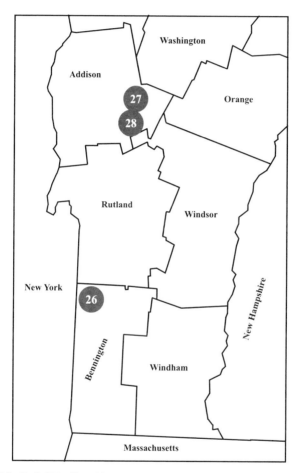

26. D & H Rail Trail - Rupert, VT
27. Moss Glen Falls - Granville, VT
28. Texas Falls - Hancock, VT

26 D&H Rail Trail

Rupert, Vermont   Bennington County

Driving Directions from the South: Follow U.S. Route 7 North through Bennington, and continue north on Route 7 to Exit 4.   From there take Vermont Route 30 North through Manchester Center, Dorset, and East Rupert.

After going 9.8 miles from the exit, turn left onto Route 315 West. Drive for 6 miles into Rupert where you will find a sign for a Junction with Route 153. Go straight onto Route 153 South. Hebron Road is 0.7 miles from this junction and goes to the right. The D&H Rail Trail is just barely up Hebron Road and goes to the right and left. There is room to park off the road near the entrance.

What to Expect: The trails are not paved, but they have a combination of small black coal-like stones and grass. There are often many birds near the trail to the right. There are almost no mosquitoes on these trails, but on occasion there are a few small biting black flies.

There is no fee as it is a trail beside the road. People ride bicycles on these trails, but no motorized vehicles are allowed. Hunting, shooting and trapping are prohibited.

There are no rest rooms. However, there is a sign about 1 mile or so further on Route 153 South pointing to the Rupert Town Office on East Street. There is a rest room in this building that can be used when the office is open. There is also a store in the same area on Route 153 South that may let hikers use their rest room.

Trail Information: The D&H Rail Trail crosses Hebron Road, so I went in both directions listing the wildflowers I saw blooming beside the trail. Trail to the right from Hebron Road or Trail to the left from Hebron Road refers to the trail that goes to the right or left as you are looking down Hebron Road from Route 153.

The trails are not marked by trail markers, but the trail is marked at the entrance and since it used to have a railroad track, the trail is obvious.

The trails are flat and quite sunny with a few trees here and there. As a result, many flowers bloom beside the trails during the Summer.

The trail to the right crosses several farm roads, passes an old train station and a pond. I turned around past the pond where there was a very short road to a highway. If you go on the trail to the right as far as I went, it is about one mile each way and takes about one hour round trip if done at a medium speed without stopping.

The trail to the left crosses a bridge at the beginning and then goes quite a way before there is another bridge. I turned around at the second bridge. If you turn around at the second bridge as I did, the trail is about 0.8 miles one way and takes about 40 minutes round trip if done at a medium speed without stopping.

Nearby Waterfalls listed in this book: Shelving Rock Falls in Fort Ann, New York; also Moss Glen Falls in Granville and Texas Falls In Hancock both in Vermont

27 Moss Glen Falls

Granville, Vermont   Addison County

See Picture No. 58VT.

<u>Driving Directions from the South</u>: Follow Route 100 North into Hancock. There you will find a junction with Route 125 which goes to the left. Continue straight on Route 100 for 7 miles past the junction with Route 125. There you will see a sign for the falls on the right. The falls are located on the left side of the road and are visible from the highway. You will find a parking lot on the left just beyond the falls.

<u>What to Expect</u>: The parking area has room for about 7 cars. The waterfalls do not come straight down, so there is a lot of splashing from rock to rock which adds to the beauty of the falls. These falls are higher than many other waterfalls I have seen in this area (probably about 45 feet).

There is no entrance fee and there are no rest rooms. I listed wildflowers that I saw along the boardwalk when I was there as well as leaves of wildflowers that would bloom earlier or later in the season.

<u>Trail Information</u>: The trail to Moss Glen Falls is only 200 feet long and consists of a bridge going over the river, a wide smooth area, and a boardwalk with a railing from which to view the falls. The walkway is wheelchair accessible.

<u>Nearby Waterfalls and Trails with Wildflowers listed in this book</u>: Texas Falls in Hancock, and D&H Rail Trail (both in Vermont); also Shelving Rock Falls in Fort Ann, New York

28 Texas Falls

Green Mountain National Forest
Hancock, Vermont   Addison County

See Picture No. 59VT.

Driving Directions from the South: Follow Route 100 North into Hancock, Vermont. At the junction with Route 125 turn left and follow Route 125 West for about 3 miles. Then turn right onto the road indicated by a Green Mountain Forest sign for Texas Falls. Drive 0.7 miles to a parking area across from the falls. There are several parking areas, so if that area is filled, go up the road to another one.

Driving Directions from the North, South, or West: From the junction of Route 7 and Vermont Route 125 in East Middlebury, turn onto Route 125 going east. Drive on Route 125 for about 13.5 miles and look for a Green Mountain Forest sign for Texas Falls. Turn left and drive 0.7 miles to a parking area across from the falls. There are several parking areas, so if that area is filled, go up the road to another one.

What to Expect: The waterfalls at Texas Falls are part of Texas Brook. They consist of three separate falls - a double falls, single falls, and another double falls. Each of them is separated by a large circular pool of swirling water.

The picture in this book shows part of the falls. As you can see, the waterfalls flow through a narrow ravine which has sheer sides created by the water flow.

The water in the river is quite clear. The area near the falls has many rocks covered with moss - an unusual look for the state of Vermont.

There are picnic tables in several places - most beyond the first parking lot. There are several trails and also pit toilets.

Trail Information: The falls are directly across the road from the first parking lot. There are signs directing you to the falls. You can see the top of the falls from the entrance path.

There are two lookouts to see more of the falls and to get pictures. One lookout is a bridge over the falls where you can look up at part of the falls. The path to this bridge is made of stone steps that are cemented together. There are sturdy wooden railings on the sides of these steps.

The second lookout is down near the bottom of the falls. The path to this lookout is similar to a regular trail.

Nearby Waterfalls and Trails with Wildflowers listed in this book: Moss Glen Falls in Granville and D&H Rail Trail in Rupert (both in Vermont); also Shelving Rock Falls in Fort Ann, New York

WILDFLOWERS IN BLOOM

Connecticut

Beginning of May

Kent Falls

Kent Falls State Park
Kent, CT   Litchfield County

See Driving Directions, What to Expect,
and Trail Information.

Late Season

Path to trail: Common Shadbush, Coltsfoot

Kent Falls Trail: Coltsfoot, Round-lobed Hepatica [Liverleaf] (white, purple, light bluish-purple, medium purple), Wake-robin [Birthroot, Purple or Red Trillium] (beginning to bloom)

Campbells Falls

Campbells Falls State Park
North Norfolk, CT   Litchfield County and
Southfield, MA   Berkshire County

See Driving Directions, What to Expect,
and Trail Information.

Late Season

Trail down to the falls: Wake-robin [Birthroot, Purple or Red

Trillium] (quite a few in one spot), American Fly Honeysuckle, Miterwort [Bishop's Cap]

Rocks near falls: Violet (yellow), Shadbush

Short trail to left just before falls: Violet (light blue)

Trail to left of parking lot (looking from road): Wake-robin [Birthroot, Purple or Red Trillium], Blue Cohosh (purple flower), Trout Lily [Yellow Adder's Tongue] (three)

Turn around after crossing three bridges and going up some steps that lead to the top of a small hill.

Middle of May

Kent Falls

Kent Falls State Park
Kent, CT   Litchfield County

See Driving Directions, What to Expect,
and Trail Information.

Late Season

Path to trail (area mowed): Apple tree, Violet (most purple, some light purple), Cuckooflower [Lady's Smock], Miterwort [Bishop's Cap], Coltsfoot, Toothwort [Crinkleroot]

Kent Falls Trail: White Baneberry [Doll's Eyes], Coltsfoot (quite a few), Early Meadow Rue, Miterwort [Bishop's Cap] (one), Wild Columbine (beginning to bloom - few), Violet (light blue, yellow - few), Bellwort (beginning to bloom), Wake-robin [Birthroot, Purple or Red Trillium], Wild Ginger, Wild Sarsaparilla (beginning to bloom)

<u>Go back down, turn right toward lower falls, then walk downstream on grass near the brook. Pass covered bridge and continue to other bridge with handrails</u>: Red Clover, Violet (white, purple, light bluish-purple, yellow), Ground Ivy [Gill-over-the-ground]

End of May

Campbells Falls

Campbells Falls State Park
North Norfolk, CT   Litchfield County and
Southfield, MA   Berkshire County

See Driving Directions, What to Expect,
and Trail Information.

Late Season

<u>Parking lot</u>: Striped Maple tree

<u>Trail down to falls</u>: Golden Alexanders, Violet (purple), Foamflower [False Miterwort] (many in spots), Baneberry, Ground Ivy [Gill-over-the-ground], Yellow Clintonia [Bluebead], Canada Mayflower [Wild Lily-of-the-valley] (beginning to bloom), Wake-robin [Birthroot, Purple or Red Trillium] (near end of bloom), Starflower (beginning to bloom), Jack-in-the-pulpit [Indian Turnip], Wild Columbine (in rocks), Violet (yellow, medium purple, white)

Short trail to left just before falls: Small-flowered Crowfoot, Golden Alexanders, Violet (yellow, medium purple, light blue - quite a few), Strawberry (few), Wild Geranium [Spotted Cranesbill] (beginning to bloom), Foamflower [False Miterwort], Miterwort [Bishop's Cap], Dwarf Raspberry, Toothwort [Crinkleroot]

Trail to left of parking lot (looking from road): Foamflower [False Miterwort] (quite a few), Jack-in-the-pulpit [Indian Turnip] (quite a few), Golden Alexanders, Miterwort [Bishop's Cap], Wake-robin [Birthroot, Purple or Red Trillium] (near end of bloom), Canada Mayflower [Wild Lily-of-the-valley] (beginning to bloom), Yellow Clintonia [Bluebead], Hairy Solomon's Seal (look under the leaves), Starflower, Wild Geranium [Spotted Cranesbill], Small-flowered Crowfoot

Same trail going into field (wet in places - especially at the beginning): Common Cinquefoil, Ragged Robin [Cuckooflower] (few), Buttercup, Red Clover, Robin's Plantain (many), Bluets [Quaker Ladies, Innocence] (many), Round-leaved Ragwort, Chokecherry, Golden Alexanders, Wild Geranium [Spotted Cranesbill], Strawberry

Beginning of June

Kent Falls

Kent Falls State Park
Kent, CT　　Litchfield County

See Driving Directions, What to Expect, and Trail Information.

Late Season

Over wooden bridge, up blacktop sidewalk, and continue past
the sidewalk to the left near the unmowed area:
Thimbleberry [Black Raspberry] (many), Common
Blackberry (few), Bristly Sarsaparilla (quite a few), Violet
(medium blue), Morrow's Honeysuckle, Buttercup, Violet
(purple)

Up Kent Falls Trail: Golden Alexanders, False Solomon's
Seal [Wild Spikenard], Canada Mayflower [Wild Lily-of-the-
valley], Round-leaved Ragwort (quite a few in two places),
Sweet Cicely, Robin's Plantain (beginning to bloom),
Clustered Snakeroot, Violet (purple, medium blue), Hooked
Crowfoot, Violet (white - few), Wild Ginger, Tartarian
Honeysuckle

Back down the trail, to the right, past the lower falls and
downstream - wildflowers not seen before: Wild Geranium
[Spotted Cranesbill], Golden Alexanders, Buttercup,
Morrow's Honeysuckle (near end of bloom), Red Clover,
Common Blackberry, Dame's Violet [Dame's Rocket]

Past covered bridge: Yellow Iris, Ground Ivy [Gill-over-the-
ground], Oxeye Daisy (beginning to bloom - few), Blue Flag
Iris, Dwarf Cinquefoil, Common Cinquefoil

Cross bridge with handrails.

Campbells Falls

Campbells Falls State Park
North Norfolk, CT   Litchfield County and
Southfield, MA   Berkshire County

See Driving Directions, What to Expect,
and Trail Information.

Late Season

Parking lot: Strawberry, False Solomon's Seal [Wild Spikenard] (beginning to bloom), Celandine, Canada Mayflower [Wild Lily-of-the-valley], Small-flowered Crowfoot, Wild Geranium [Spotted Cranesbill], Ragged Robin [Cuckooflower], Golden Alexanders, Buttercup, Thyme-leaved Speedwell, Ground Ivy [Gill-over-the-ground], Violet (yellow)

Trail down to falls: Buttercup, Wild Geranium [Spotted Cranesbill], Ground Ivy [Gill-over-the-ground], Strawberry, Foamflower [False Miterwort] (big patch), Starflower (one), Yellow Clintonia [Bluebead] (near end of bloom), Jack-in-the-pulpit [Indian Turnip], White Baneberry [Doll's Eyes], Canada Mayflower [Wild Lily-of-the-valley], Hairy Solomon's Seal (look under the leaves), Violet (medium bluish-purple)

Short trail to left just before the falls: Golden Alexanders, Strawberry, Violet (medium purple, light purple), Wild Geranium [Spotted Cranesbill], Jack-in-the-pulpit [Indian Turnip], Foamflower [False Miterwort], Common Wood Sorrel, Canada Mayflower [Wild Lily-of-the-valley] (one), Baneberry

Trail to left of parking lot (looking from road): Foamflower [False Miterwort] (near end of bloom), Canada Mayflower [Wild Lily-of-the-valley] (many), Jack-in-the-pulpit [Indian Turnip], Wild Geranium [Spotted Cranesbill], Golden Alexanders, Miterwort [Bishop's Cap] (near end of bloom), False Solomon's Seal [Wild Spikenard], Wild Sarsaparilla, Indian Cucumber Root (look under the leaves), Small-flowered Crowfoot

Same trail into field: Ragged Robin [Cuckooflower] (quite a few in spots), Buttercup, Robin's Plantain (many in spots), Common Cinquefoil, Red Clover, Common Speedwell, Field Hawkweed [King Devil] (many in spots), Bluets [Quaker Ladies, Innocence], Orange Hawkweed [Devil's Paintbrush], Blue-eyed Grass, Round-leaved Ragwort, Strawberry, Wild Geranium [Spotted Cranesbill], Oxeye Daisy (beginning to bloom), Lesser Stitchwort

Middle of June

Prydden Brook Falls

Paugusett State Forest
Newtown, CT   Fairfield County

See Driving Directions, What to Expect,
and Trail Information.

Wildflowers and wildflower leaves seen along the trail to the falls: Canada Mayflower [Wild Lily-of-the-valley] (leaves), Maple-leaved Viburnum [Dockmackie], Field Hawkweed [King Devil], Common Cinquefoil, Common Blackberry (one), Bloodroot (leaf), Mountain Laurel (beginning to bloom - mostly buds), Jack-in-the-pulpit [Indian Turnip] (leaves),

Common Speedwell, Starflower (leaves), Indian Cucumber Root (one bloom), Trillium (finished blooming), Spotted Touch-me-not [Jewelweed] (leaves), Striped [Spotted] Wintergreen (buds)

End of June

Kent Falls

Kent Falls State Park
Kent, CT   Litchfield County

See Driving Directions, What to Expect,
and Trail Information.

Late Season

Over bridge with wooden handrails: Yellow Iris, Blue Flag Iris, Yellow Wood Sorrel, Red Clover

Up blacktop sidewalk to the end and left beside unmowed area: Multiflora Rose, Buttercup, Thimbleberry [Black Raspberry], Daisy Fleabane [Sweet Scabious], Purple-flowering Raspberry, Common [Philadelphia] Fleabane, Bristly Sarsaparilla

Up Kent Falls Trail: Common Speedwell, Robin's Plantain, Common [Philadelphia] Fleabane, Field Hawkweed [King Devil], Clustered Snakeroot

Back down the trail, to the right, past the lower falls, and downstream: Some flowers seen before plus Common Blackberry (near end of bloom), Dame's Violet [Dame's Rocket]

.

Through covered bridge and continuing downstream: Sweet William, Yellow-poplar Tuliptree, Panicled [Gray] Dogwood, Oxeye Daisy, Garden Lupine, Rough-fruited [Sulphur] Cinquefoil, Ground Ivy [Gill-over-the-ground]

Campbells Falls

Campbells Falls State Park
North Norfolk, CT   Litchfield County and
Southfield, MA   Berkshire County

See Driving Directions, What to Expect,
and Trail Information.

Late Season

Near parking lot: Red Clover, Buttercup, Yellow Wood Sorrel, Common Cinquefoil (one), Wild Geranium [Spotted Cranesbill] (one - near end of bloom), Common Blackberry

Trail down to falls: Red Clover, Ground Ivy [Gill-over-the-ground], Thimbleberry [Black Raspberry], Yellow Wood Sorrel, Common Speedwell, Common Cinquefoil, Common Blackberry

Short trail to left just before falls: Wood Nettle, Buttercup, Common Blackberry (many in one place), Common Cinquefoil, Yellow Wood Sorrel, Ragged Robin [Cuckooflower], Bluets [Quaker Ladies, Innocence], Common Wood Sorrel (many), Common Speedwell

Trail to left of parking lot (looking from road): Common Blackberry, Wild Geranium [Spotted Cranesbill] (one - near end of bloom)

<u>Same trail into field</u>: Red Clover (quite a few), Multiflora Rose, Yarrow [Milfoil], Buttercup, Common Cinquefoil, Lesser Stitchwort, Selfheal [Heal-all], Ragged Robin [Cuckooflower] (almost finished), Oxeye Daisy (quite a few), Yellow Wood Sorrel, Smaller Forget-me-not, Field Hawkweed [King Devil] (many in the shade - near end of bloom in the sun), Daisy Fleabane [Sweet Scabious], Panicled [Gray] Dogwood, Robin's Plantain (finished in the sun, near end in the shade), Common Blackberry (near end of bloom), Orange Hawkweed [Devil's Paintbrush] (near end of bloom except in the shade), Bluets [Quaker Ladies, Innocence] (near end of bloom), Common Speedwell, Blue-eyed Grass (one), Spiked Lobelia (quite a few in one spot), Black-eyed Susan

Middle of July

Kent Falls

Kent Falls State Park
Kent, CT   Litchfield County

See Driving Directions, What to Expect,
and Trail Information.

Late Season

<u>Bridge with wooden handrails</u>: Purple Loosestrife, Oxeye Daisy, Spotted Joe-Pye Weed (beginning to bloom), Tall Meadow Rue

<u>Up blacktop sidewalk to the end and left beside unmowed area</u>:   Canada Lily (one), White Avens, Enchanter's Nightshade, Yellow Wood Sorrel, Wild Basil, Selfheal [Heal-all]

Up and down Kent Falls Trail: Daisy Fleabane [Sweet Scabious], Thimbleweed [Tall Anemone] (most finished), Agrimony

Right toward lower falls and left following brook downstream: Agrimony, Fringed Loosestrife (quite a few), Tall Meadow Rue, Thimbleweed [Tall Anemone], Red Clover, Cow [Tufted] Vetch, Daisy Fleabane [Sweet Scabious], Common St. Johnswort, Wild Carrot [Queen Anne's Lace, Bird's Nest]

Through covered bridge and continuing downstream: Sweet William, Black-eyed Susan

End of July

Campbells Falls

Campbells Falls State Park
North Norfolk, Connecticut   Litchfield County and
Southfield, Massachusetts   Berkshire County

See Driving Directions, What to Expect,
and Trail Information.

Late Season

Wildflowers by parking lot: Selfheal [Heal-all], Daisy Fleabane [Sweet Scabious], Buttercup, Spotted Touch-me-not [Jewelweed] (beginning to bloom), Yellow Wood Sorrel, Agrimony, Fringed Loosestrife, Enchanter's Nightshade

Trail down to falls: Daisy Fleabane [Sweet Scabious], Selfheal [Heal-all], Red Clover, Agrimony, Spreading Dogbane, Spotted Touch-me-not [Jewelweed], Enchanter's Nightshade, Tall Nettle

Short trail to left just before falls: Wood Nettle, Buttercup, Selfheal [Heal-all], White Avens

Trail to left of parking lot (looking from road):   Oxeye Daisy, Enchanter's Nightshade, White Avens

Same trail into field: Oxeye Daisy, Selfheal [Heal-all], Red Clover, Wild Carrot [Queen Anne's Lace, Bird's Nest], Common St. Johnswort,   Buttercup, Fringed Loosestrife, Yarrow [Milfoil], Ragged Robin [Cuckooflower] (one), Lesser Stitchwort, Yellow Wood Sorrel, Daisy Fleabane [Sweet Scabious], Black-eyed Susan, Canada Lily [Meadow Lily, Wild Yellow Lily] (two), Swamp Candles [Yellow Loosestrife], Spotted Joe-Pye Weed, Orange Hawkweed [Devil's Paintbrush] (two), Spotted Touch-me-not [Jewelweed] (beginning to bloom), Meadowsweet, Common Evening Primrose (one), Goldenrod (beginning to bloom), Spiked Lobelia, Deptford Pink (one)

Beginning of August

Kent Falls

Kent Falls State Park
Kent, CT   Litchfield County

See Driving Directions, What to Expect,
and Trail Information.

Late Season

Near parking area: Spotted Touch-me-not [Jewelweed], Bouncing Bet [Soapwort], Purple Loosestrife, Spotted Joe-Pye Weed, Boneset [Thoroughwort], Goldenrod

Bridge with wooden handrails: Tall [Green-headed] Coneflower, Agrimony, Yellow Wood Sorrel

Up blacktop sidewalk to the end and left beside unmowed area: Nipplewort, Fringed Loosestrife, Purple-flowering Raspberry, White Avens, Enchanter's Nightshade, Virgin's Bower, Selfheal [Heal-all], Spiked Lobelia (one)

Past entrance to Kent Falls Trail: Zigzag [Broad-leaved] Goldenrod (beginning to bloom), Red Clover

Down steps and to the left following brook downstream: Wild Carrot [Queen Anne's Lace, Bird's Nest], White Snakeroot, Meadowsweet, Daisy Fleabane [Sweet Scabious], Common Burdock, Pale-leaved Sunflower, Flat-topped Aster (one - beginning to bloom), Horse Balm [Richweed, Stoneroot], Common St. Johnswort (near end of bloom), Common Evening Primrose, Hedge Bindweed (white)

Past covered bridge and then across bridge with handrails: Great [Star] Chickweed, Peppermint, Black-eyed Susan, Swamp Milkweed, Purple Coneflower

End of August

Kent Falls

Kent Falls State Park
Kent, CT   Litchfield County

See Driving Directions, What to Expect,
and Trail Information.

Late Season

<u>Near parking lot and bridge with handrails</u>:   Purple Loosestrife, Goldenrod, Spotted Touch-me-not [Jewelweed], Spotted Joe-Pye Weed (near end of bloom), Swamp Rose Mallow (pink), Boneset [Thoroughwort], Tall [Green-headed] Coneflower, Wild Carrot [Queen Anne's Lace, Bird's Nest], Red Clover, Agrimony (near end of bloom), Yellow Wood Sorrel

<u>Up blacktop sidewalk to the end and left beside unmowed area</u>:   Nipplewort, Selfheal [Heal-all], Purple-flowering Raspberry, Common Burdock, White Wood Aster, Enchanter's Nightshade, Zigzag [Broad-leaved] Goldenrod, Blue-stemmed [Wreath] Goldenrod

<u>Up Kent Falls Trail</u>:   White Wood Aster (many), Daisy Fleabane [Sweet Scabious], Spiked Lobelia, Selfheal [Heal-all], Goldenrod, Zigzag [Broad-leaved] Goldenrod, Great Lobelia, White Snakeroot, Hog Peanut

<u>Back down the trail and to the right</u>: Great [Star] Chickweed, White Campion (near end of bloom), White Snakeroot

<u>Past lower falls and to the left, following the brook downstream</u>:   Spiked Lobelia, Pale-leaved Sunflower, Bouncing Bet [Soapwort], Flat-topped Aster, Fringed Loosestrife, Hedge Bindweed (white), Common St. Johnswort, Common Evening Primrose

<u>Past covered bridge and across bridge with handrails</u>: Purple-stemmed Aster, Arrow-leaved Tearthumb, Peppermint, Monkey Flower, Purple Coneflower

Beginning of September

Kent Falls

Kent Falls State Park
Kent, CT   Litchfield County

See Driving Directions, What to Expect,
and Trail Information.

Late Season

<u>By parking lot and bridge with wooden handrails</u>:   Purple Loosestrife, Purple Coneflower, Goldenrod, Chicory, Spotted Knapweed, Swamp Rose Mallow

<u>Blacktop sidewalk to the end and left beside unmowed area</u>: Common Evening Primrose, Great [Star] Chickweed, Purple-stemmed Aster (beginning to bloom), Yellow Wood Sorrel, Daisy Fleabane [Sweet Scabious], Selfheal [Heal-all], Tall Nettle, Pale-leaved Sunflower, Horse Balm [Richweed, Stoneroot], Red Clover, Panicled Aster (beginning to bloom),

White Wood Aster (many up Kent Falls Trail), Zigzag [Broad-leaved] Goldenrod (beginning to bloom - many up Kent Falls Trail)

Up Kent Falls Trail: Flowers not mentioned before: Boott's Rattlesnake Root, White Snakeroot, Spiked Lobelia (near end of bloom), Hog Peanut (pale purple, white), Great Lobelia, Heart-leaved Aster, Schreber's Aster

Back down trail, turn right to lower falls, then left following the brook downstream. Flowers not listed before: Wood Nettle, Bouncing Bet [Soapwort], Common Evening Primrose

Past covered bridge: Agrimony, Common Burdock, Spotted Joe-Pye Weed (near end of bloom), Boneset [Thoroughwort] (near end of bloom)

Over bridge with handrails.

End of September

Dean's Ravine

Housatonic State Forest
Canaan, CT   Litchfield County

See Driving Directions, What to Expect,
and Trail Information.

Late Season

Trail to falls: White Wood Aster, Blue-stemmed [Wreath] Goldenrod, Zigzag [Broad-leaved] Goldenrod, Calico [Starved] Aster, Tall White Lettuce

Pine Swamp Brook Falls

Sharon, CT   Litchfield County

Wildflowers near Route 7: No flowers at this time.

Beginning of October

Kent Falls

Kent Falls State Park
Kent, CT   Litchfield County

See Driving Directions, What to Expect,
and Trail Information.

Early Season

Over bridge with handrails, up the blacktop sidewalk, and to the left at the edge of the mowed area: Heart-leaved Aster (white, light purple), Calico [Starved] Aster, Panicled Aster, Daisy Fleabane [Sweet Scabious], Purple-stemmed Aster, Selfheal [Heal-all], Zigzag [Broad-leaved] Goldenrod, White Wood Aster, Chicory, Great [Star] Chickweed

Up and back down Kent Falls Trail: White Wood Aster, Purple-stemmed Aster, Zigzag [Broad-leaved] Goldenrod, Heart-leaved Aster, Blue-stemmed [Wreath] Goldenrod, Panicled Aster, Schreber's Aster, Tall White Lettuce

To the right after Kent Falls Trail and following the brook downstream: Bouncing Bet [Soapwort], Gray-headed Coneflower, Wild Carrot [Queen Anne's Lace, Bird's Nest], Black-eyed Susan

Massachusetts

Middle of April

The Norcross Wildlife Sanctuary at Tupper Hill

Monson and Wales, MA   Hampden County

See Driving Directions, What to Expect,
and Trail Information.

Late Season

Start by leaving the Visitors Center from the left side door. At the end of the sidewalk turn right and then turn left toward the Short Trail. Enter the gate to the fenced-in Short Trail area: Bloodroot, Rue Anemone, Snow Trillium (near end of bloom), White Trout Lily [White Adder's Tongue], Twinleaf (buds)

Go out other gate and continue on trails described in Trail Information: Skunk Cabbage

Turn right into Circle Garden: Trailing Arbutus [Mayflower], Oconee Bells

Lime Flower Cobbles: Sharp-lobed Hepatica (white and very light pink), Round-lobed Hepatica [Liverleaf] (white), Toad Trillium [Toadshade] (maroon), White Trout Lily [White Adder's Tongue] (beginning to bloom), Dutchman's Breeches (beginning to bloom), Rue Anemone

Continue back to Visitors Center: Daffodil [Narcissus]

End of April

High Ledges Wildlife Sanctuary

Shelburne, MA   Franklin County

See Driving Directions, What to Expect,
and Trail Information.

Late Season

The entry road will be closed. Walk from beginning of road
to trails. Road past gate after parking lot: Pussy Willow
(some going to seed), Trailing Arbutus [Mayflower] (few)

Continue on trail as explained in trail directions: Trailing
Arbutus [Mayflower]

Mount Sugarloaf State Reservation

South Deerfield, MA   Franklin County

See Driving Directions, What to Expect,
and Trail Information.

Late Season

Trail from lower parking lot: Round-lobed Hepatica
[Liverleaf] (white, light purple)

Fork to left: Trailing Arbutus [Mayflower] (few)

Road to right downhill - left cliff: Coltsfoot, Trailing Arbutus
[Mayflower], Round-lobed Hepatica [Liverleaf] (light purple,
light pink)

Sanderson Brook Falls

Chester-Blandford State Forest
Chester and Blandford, MA   Hampden County

See Driving Directions, What to Expect,
and Trail Information.

Late Season

Sanderson Brook Road after crossing the three bridges: Violet (yellow)

Path to waterfall (turn right at blue arrow): Nothing blooming yet.

Chapelbrook Falls

Chapelbrook Reservation
South Ashfield, MA   Franklin County

See Driving Directions, What to Expect,
and Trail Information.

Early Season

Along the road into the reservation - stopped at three large rocks: Hobblebush, Violet (yellow), Wake-robin [Birthroot, Purple or Red Trillium]

Beginning of May

Bash Bish Falls

Bash Bish Falls State Park
Mount Washington, MA   Berkshire County

See Driving Directions, What to Expect,
and Trail Information.

Late Season

Trail to the falls: Early Meadow Rue (beginning to bloom),
Wake-robin [Birthroot, Purple or Red Trillium], Bloodroot,
Early Saxifrage (beginning to bloom - quite a few), American
Fly Honeysuckle, Coltsfoot, Bluets [Quaker Ladies,
Innocence] (beginning to bloom)

The Norcross Wildlife Sanctuary at Tupper Hill

Monson and Wales, MA   Hampden County

See Driving Directions, What to Expect,
and Trail Information.

Early Season

Start by leaving the Visitors Center from the left side door. At
the end of the sidewalk, turn right and then turn left into the
Hickory Grove toward the Short Trail: Bluets [Quaker Ladies,
Innocence], Violet (blue)

Short Trail (through gate to fenced-in area): Pinkshell Azalea,
Virginia Bluebells [Virginia Cowslip], Rue Anemone,
Goldenseal [Orangeroot], Carolina Spring Beauty, Spring
Beauty, Violet (yellow), Round-leaved Ragwort, Myrtle

[Periwinkle], Toad Trillium [Toadshade], Large-flowered [Great White] Trillium (white), Wake-robin [Birthroot, Purple or Red Trillium], Wood Anemone [Windflower,] Wild Bleeding Heart, Violet (light bluish-purple), Wild Blue Phlox, Redbud (near end of bloom), Toothwort [Crinkleroot], Ozark Trillium, Blue Cohosh (yellow), Prairie Trillium, Rue Anemone

Gate out of wildflower garden (Short Trail) and into Conifer Grove: Bluets [Quaker Ladies, Innocence], Dwarf Ginseng, Dwarf Cinquefoil, Pink Rock Cress, Violet (blue), Shadbush

Upland Shrub Area: Early Low Blueberry, Shadbush, Bluets [Quaker Ladies, Innocence], Dwarf Cinquefoil, Dwarf Ginseng

Lower Trail: Marsh Marigold [Cowslip], Early Low Blueberry, Highbush [Swamp] Blueberry, Violet (blue)

Right at Boardwalk: Violet (light purple)

Pond Trail (go to right around pond): Swamp Pink [Swamp Hyacinth], Cleft Phlox [Sand Phlox], Bluestar (beginning to bloom), Dwarf [Vernal] Iris, Corn Speedwell, Dwarf Cinquefoil, Prairie Smoke

Lime Flower Cobbles: Rue Anemone, Violet (purple), Spring Beauty (many), Dutchman's Breeches, Carolina Spring Beauty, Goldthread, Shadbush, Spreading Globeflower, [Globeflower], Toothwort [Crinkleroot], Marsh Marigold [Cowslip], Dwarf Ginseng, Blue Cohosh (greenish-yellow), Violet (yellow, purple, white), White Trillium, Rue Anemone, Trout Lily [Yellow Adder's Tongue] (one), Golden Ragwort, Wild Blue Phlox, Virginia Bluebells [Virginia Cowslip], Shadbush, Violet (blue)

Field next to Lime Flower Cobbles: Apple tree, Smaller Pussytoes, Dwarf Cinquefoil, Crab Apple tree, Flowering Dogwood

Pine Barren Area: Highbush [Swamp] Blueberry, Bluets [Quaker Ladies, Innocence], Pixie Moss, Early Low Blueberry, Dwarf Cinquefoil

Go back to Lower Trail and take bridge to the left to Visitors Center.

Sanderson Brook Falls

Chester-Blandford State Forest
Chester and Blandford, MA   Hampden County

See Driving Directions, What to Expect,
and Trail Information.

Late Season

Sanderson Brook Road: Wake-robin [Birthroot, Purple or Red Trillium], Violet (white, purple), Hobblebush (many in one spot), Squirrel Corn, Dutchman's Breeches, Violet (light bluish-purple), Trout Lily [Yellow Adder's Tongue] (one), Violet (yellow), Wild Ginger

Path to falls (turn right at blue arrow): No new flowers

High Ledges Wildlife Sanctuary

Shelburne, MA   Franklin County

See Driving Directions, What to Expect,
and Trail Information.

Early Season

Road from parking lot past gate: Apple tree, Early Low Blueberry, Violet (bluish-purple), Shadbush (near end of bloom)

Right on Lady's Slipper Trail (second sign): Sessile-leaved Bellwort [Wild Oats], Violet (bluish-purple), Hobblebush

Across Spring Brook: Early Saxifrage, Violet (yellow, white with purple lines near center), Miterwort [Bishop's Cap], Dwarf Ginseng, Jack-in-the-pulpit [Indian Turnip], Wake-robin [Birthroot, Purple or Red Trillium], Violet (very light purple), Marsh Marigold [Cowslip]

Turn left after bridge: No new flowers were observed.

Turn right soon after that: No new flowers were observed.

Turn left onto road: No new flowers were observed.

Mount Sugarloaf State Reservation

South Deerfield, MA   Franklin County

See Driving Directions, What to Expect,
and Trail Information.

Early Season

Trail going up the mountain beginning at the lower parking lot: Chokecherry, Bluets [Quaker Ladies, Innocence], Creeping Bluets, Strawberry (quite a few in places), Flowering Dogwood (quite a few), Jack-in-the-pulpit [Indian Turnip]

<u>Bear right at fork</u>: Common Winter Cress [Yellow Rocket], Early Meadow Rue, Dwarf Cinquefoil, Violet (purple)

<u>Bear left at fork</u>: Fringed Polygala [Flowering Wintergreen, Gaywings]

<u>Follow sign for summit.   Turn right at road (going downhill).</u>
<u>Left side of road</u>: Violet (dark purple with two white spots)

<u>Follow "Trail" sign past "Do Not Enter" sign:</u> Bluets [Quaker Ladies, Innocence], Violet (purple)

Middle of May

Bash Bish Falls

Bash Bish Falls State Park
Mount Washington, MA   Berkshire County

See Driving Directions, What to Expect,
and Trail Information.

Late Season

<u>Flowers by the parking lot</u>:   Magnolia tree (beginning to bloom)

<u>Trail to falls</u>:   Hairy Solomon's Seal (quite a few), Early Saxifrage (many in spots), Small-flowered Crowfoot (near end of bloom), Wake-robin [Birthroot, Purple or Red Trillium] (near end of bloom), Bellwort (beginning to bloom), Wild Sarsaparilla (beginning to bloom), Violet (yellow), Early Meadow Rue (near end of bloom), Wood Betony [Lousewort] (few), Bluets [Quaker Ladies, Innocence] (many in one area),

Violet (purple), Baneberry (beginning to bloom), Jack-in-the-pulpit [Indian Turnip] (few), Wild Black Currant (few)

Mount Greylock State Reservation

Cheshire and New Ashford, MA   Berkshire County

See Driving Directions, What to Expect,
and Trail Information.

Late Season

Jones Nose Trail through field: Violet (purple), Strawberry (quite a few), Smooth Shadbush (quite a few), Bird [Pin, Fire] Cherry (beginning to bloom), Early Low Blueberry, Early Saxifrage, Red-berried Elder

Woods: Violet (purple), Wake-robin [Birthroot, Purple or Red Trillium] (many in spots), Red-berried Elder, Dutchman's Breeches (few - near end of bloom), Jack-in-the-pulpit [Indian Turnip], Small-flowered Crowfoot (few), Trout Lily [Yellow Adder's Tongue] (many in spots), Hobblebush (scattered here and there), Carolina Spring Beauty, Sessile-leaved Bellwort [Wild Oats] (few)

CCC Dynamite Foot and Ski Trail to left: Blue Cohosh (near end of bloom), Violet (white), Marsh Marigold [Cowslip]

Turned around at a small stream with a rock to cross it and a very small waterfall to the right..

End of May

High Ledges Wildlife Sanctuary

Shelburne, MA   Franklin County

See Driving Directions, What to Expect,
and Trail Information.

Early Season

Entrance road: Lilac, Common Winter Cress [Yellow Rocket], Strawberry, Common Cinquefoil, Early Low Blueberry, Apple tree, Sessile-leaved Bellwort [Wild Oats], Violet (bluish-purple, purple, light purple), Early Saxifrage, Dwarf Cinquefoil, Bluets [Quaker Ladies, Innocence], Wild Columbine

Past vernal pool and left at fork in the road: Bird [Pin or Fire] Cherry (many in one spot)

Past cabin - (do not turn left): Wild Columbine, Early Low Blueberry, Pink Lady's Slipper [Moccasin Flower] (beginning to bloom), Sessile-leaved Bellwort [Wild Oats]

Lady's Slipper Trail: Violet (yellow), Miterwort [Bishop's Cap]

Follow Lady's Slipper Trail to the right: Early Saxifrage (one), Wild Sarsaparilla (beginning to bloom), Jack-in-the-pulpit [Indian Turnip], Violet (purple, light purple), Wake-robin [Birthroot, Purple or Red Trillium] (near end of bloom), Foamflower [False Miterwort], Dwarf Ginseng (few), Violet (white with purple lines in center), Toothwort [Crinkleroot], Violet (medium blue)

After bridge go immediately to left and follow yellow markers back to road. Turn left at road. This will lead you back to the parking lot.

Mount Sugarloaf State Reservation

South Deerfield, MA   Franklin County

See Driving Directions, What the Expect,
and Trail Information.

Early Season

Trail from lower parking lot: Chokecherry, Wild Geranium [Spotted Cranesbill], Common Cinquefoil, Common Winter Cress [Yellow Rocket], Corn Speedwell, Shepherd's Purse, Thimbleberry [Black Raspberry], Strawberry, Jack-in-the-pulpit [Indian Turnip], White Baneberry [Doll's Eyes], Flowering Dogwood, Canada Mayflower [Wild Lily-of-the-valley]

Go left at fork: Fringed Polygala [Flowering Wintergreen or Gaywings] (few), Pink Lady's Slipper [Moccasin Flower] (two), Dwarf Cinquefoil

Follow sign towards summit. Turn right at road (going downhill) - flowers on left side of road : Pink Azalea [Pinxter Flower], Bluets [Quaker Ladies, Innocence], Coltsfoot (one), Fringed Polygala [Flowering Wintergreen or Gaywings], Round-leaved Ragwort, Early Saxifrage, Wild Columbine, Jack-in-the-pulpit [Indian Turnip], Strawberry, Violet (bluish-purple), Flowering Dogwood

Chapelbrook Falls

Chapelbrook Reservation
South Ashfield, MA   Franklin County

See Driving Directions, What to Expect,
and Trail Information.

Early Season

Along the road into the reservation (going downhill) - stopped
at large rocks: Violet (white with purple lines in bottom petal
- quite a few), Violet (light purple), Golden Alexanders (one),
Wild Sarsaparilla (beginning to bloom)

Sanderson Brook Falls

Chester-Blandford State Forest
Chester and Blandford, MA   Hampden County

See Driving Directions, What to Expect,
and Trail Information.

Late Season

Sanderson Brook Road: Canada Mayflower [Wild Lily-of-
the-valley], Golden Alexanders, Strawberry, Red Baneberry,
White Baneberry [Doll's Eyes], Jack-in-the-pulpit [Indian
Turnip], Foamflower [False Miterwort], Violet (many purple,
some light purple, and small white), Toothwort [Crinkleroot],
Red-berried Elder (near end of bloom), Hooked Crowfoot,
Violet (yellow, white), Small-flowered Crowfoot, Miterwort
[Bishop's Cap], Bluets [Quaker Ladies, Innocence] (few)

Path to falls (turn right at blue arrow):   Wood Anemone
[Windflower]

Mount Greylock State Reservation

Cheshire and New Ashford, MA   Berkshire County

See Driving Directions, What to Expect,
and Trail Information.

Early Season

Jones Nose Trail through field: Strawberry, Early Low
Blueberry, Apple trees at a distance, Bird [Pin , Fire] Cherry

Woods: Wake-robin [Birthroot, Purple or Red Trillium]
(many in several spots), Violet (white with dark lines near the
center), Dutchman's Breeches (near end of bloom), Violet
(bluish-purple), Jack-in-the-pulpit [Indian Turnip], Red-
berried Elder, Hobblebush (near end of bloom), Carolina
Spring Beauty, Trout Lily [Yellow Adder's Tongue] (some
near end of bloom)

Over a little bridge: Sessile-leaved Bellwort [Wild Oats]

Turn left at fork (follow CCC Dynamite Foot and Ski Trail
sign): Foamflower [False Miterwort] (beginning to bloom),
Violet (yellow), Toothwort [Crinkleroot] (beginning to bloom)

Over stream - double log bridge: Marsh Marigold [Cowslip],
Rosybells [Rose Twisted Stalk or Rose Mandarin]

Turned around at a small stream with a rock to cross it and a
very small waterfall to the right.

Norcross Wildlife Sanctuary at Tupper Hill

Monson and Wales, MA   Hampden County

See Driving Directions, What to Expect,
and Trail Information.

Late Season

Entrance area: Wright's Viburnum, Highbush [Swamp]
Blueberry, Rhododendron (beginning to bloom), Pink Azalea
[Pinxter Flower], European Cranberry Bush, Tartarian
Honeysuckle, Jack-in-the-pulpit [Indian Turnip], Buttercup

Start by leaving the Visitors Center from the left side door.
Garden to right of sidewalk: Wild Columbine (beginning to
bloom), Siebold Viburnum (beginning to bloom)

Turn right and then left into the Hickory Grove following the
sign to the Short Trail: Buttercup, Bluets [Quaker Ladies,
Innocence], Field Pussytoes (near end of bloom), Common
Cinquefoil, Violet (medium purple), Robin's Plantain
(beginning to bloom - one), Late Low Blueberry

Short Trail through gate to fenced-in area: Great Solomon's
Seal, Large-flowered Bellwort [Great Merrybells], Wild Blue
Phlox, Creeping Phlox, Jack-in-the-pulpit [Indian Turnip]
(quite a few - scattered), Bluestar, Baneberry (beginning to
bloom), Virginia Bluebells [Virginia Cowslip] (near end of
bloom), Violet (medium blue), Wild Geranium [Spotted
Cranesbill] (quite a few - scattered), Round-leaved Ragwort,
Spring Beauty, Shooting Star, Jacob's Ladder, Crested Iris
[Dwarf Crested Iris], Rue Anemone (few), Miterwort
[Bishop's Cap] (near end of bloom), Foamflower [False
Miterwort] (many in three spots), Green Trillium, Large-
flowered [Great White] Trillium (quite a few), Wild Ginger,

Golden Alexanders, Wild Bleeding Heart (near end of bloom), Moss Phlox [Moss Pink or Ground Pink] (white), Violet (white), Larger Yellow Lady's Slipper, Rose Trillium, Bellwort (few), Yellow Trillium, Albino Purple Trillium, Golden Groundsel, Umbrella Leaf (one), Smaller Yellow Lady's Slipper, Prairie Trillium (one), Nodding Trillium, Dog Hobble, Jewel Shooting Star

Gate out of wildflower garden (Short Trail), across road, and into Conifer Grove: New flowers - Bluets [Quaker Ladies, Innocence] (many), Starflower [May Star] (many), Fringed Polygala [Flowering Wintergreen, Gaywings] (quite a few - scattered), Strawberry, Common Cinquefoil, Violet (medium blue)

Turn right after bridge and go over two boards (second bridge): Early Low Blueberry

Left at fork (do not cross bridge); go right to pond over boardwalk; then go right to pond trail: Wild Lupine (most beginning to bloom - some fairly well out), Azalea (purple), Bluestar (many), Common Winter Cress [Yellow Rocket], Cleft Phlox [Sand Phlox] (blue), Moss Phlox [Moss Pink or Ground Pink] (white)

Back to fork in boardwalk; turn right; then turn right after boardwalk into Circle Garden: Canada Mayflower [Wild Lily-of-the-valley], Starflower [May Star], Crested Iris [Dwarf Crested Iris] (purple, white), Creeping Phlox (purple), Large-flowered Trillium [Great White Trillium] (two), Nodding Trillium (one), Violet (medium purple), Herb Robert, Fringed Polygala [Flowering Wintergreen, Gaywings], Highbush [Swamp] Blueberry

Over bridge to Fern Lime Cobble area: Large-flowered Trillium [Great White Trillium] (many in one area)

To left (right of stream): White Baneberry [Doll's Eyes] (near end of bloom), Wild Geranium [Spotted Cranesbill] (few), Golden Groundsel, Robin's Plantain (few), Mayapple [Mandrake], Fire Pink, Wild Blue Phlox (quite a few), Late Low Blueberry, Rue Anemone, White Baneberry [Doll's Eyes], Canada Mayflower [Wild Lily-of-the-valley] (beginning to bloom), Dwarf Ginseng (two)

Lime Flower Cobble: Shooting Star, Rue Anemone, Large-flowered Trillium [Great White Trillium], Golden Groundsel (many in places), Violet (medium purple), Foamflower [False Miterwort], White Baneberry [Doll's Eyes], Rue Anemone, Wild Bleeding Heart, Spring Beauty (many), Golden Alexanders (one), Blue-eyed Grass (one), Smaller Yellow Lady's Slipper, Golden Star, Jack-in-the-pulpit [Indian Turnip], Violet (purple with purplish leaf), Miterwort [Bishop's Cap], Violet (yellow), Fringed Polygala [Flowering Wintergreen, Gaywings], Crested Iris [Dwarf Crested Iris]

Up steps to field: Buttercup (many)

Through Pine Barren Area - new flowers: Sand Myrtle, Purple Chokeberry, Golden Ragwort

Back to Visitors Center - left at bridge

Cascade Falls

North Adams, MA   Berkshire County

See Driving Directions, What to Expect, and Trail Information.

Late Season

<u>Trail to Cascade Falls</u>:   Morrow's Honeysuckle, Myrtle [Periwinkle], Hooked Crowfoot (quite a few), Small-flowered Crowfoot, Violet (white with purple lines going to the center - many), Jack-in-the-pulpit [Indian Turnip], Bugle, Golden Alexanders, Strawberry, Cuckooflower (Lady's Smock], Canada Mayflower [Wild Lily-of-the-valley], Baneberry, Violet (yellow - many in one place - purple), Starflower (beginning to bloom), Sweet Cicely (beginning to bloom), Foamflower [False Miterwort] (many), Round-leaved Ragwort, Golden Ragwort, Wild Sarsaparilla, False Solomon's Seal [Wild Spikenard] (just beginning to bloom), Red-berried Elder (near end of bloom), Yellow Clintonia [Bluebead], Miterwort [Bishop's Cap]

Beginning of June

Bash Bish Falls

Bash Bish Falls State Park
Mount Washington, MA   Berkshire County

See Driving Directions, What to Expect,
and Trail Information.

Late Season

<u>Trail to falls</u>: False Solomon's Seal [Wild Spikenard], Golden Alexanders (one), Hairy Solomon's Seal   (look under the leaves - few - near end of bloom), Wild Geranium [Spotted Cranesbill] (few), Maple-leaved Viburnum [Dockmackie] (buds), Sweet Cicely (few), Canada Mayflower [Wild Lily-of-the-valley] (one)

Trail above steps: Bluets [Quaker Ladies, Innocence] (many), Strawberry (few), Common Cinquefoil, Violet (purple), Small-flowered Crowfoot, Round-leaved Ragwort (many in one spot), Buttercup (one), Common [Philadelphia] Fleabane

Mount Greylock State Reservation

Cheshire and New Ashford, MA   Berkshire County

See Driving Directions, What to Expect,
and Trail Information.

Early Season

Jones Nose Trail through field: Strawberry, Morrow's Honeysuckle, Chokecherry, Common Cinquefoil, Bluets [Quaker Ladies, Innocence], Blue-eyed Grass, One-flowered Cancerroot [Ghost Pipe], Hawthorn, Early Low Blueberry

Woods: Violet (purple), Jack-in-the-pulpit [Indian Turnip], Sweet Cicely, Yellow Clintonia [Bluebead], Canada Mayflower [Wild Lily-of-the-valley] (beginning to bloom), Common Wood Sorrel (beginning to bloom), Hobblebush (near end of bloom)

Left on CCC Dynamite Trail: Foamflower [False Miterwort] (quite a few), Wake-robin [Birthroot, Purple or Red Trillium] (near end of bloom), False Solomon's Seal [Wild Spikenard] (beginning to bloom), Violet (pale purple with yellow and purple lines in center - quite a few in one spot), White Baneberry [Doll's Eyes], Buttercup, Cream-colored Avens

Continued to small stream with a rock to cross it and a very small waterfall on the right. Then turned around.

High Ledges Wildlife Sanctuary

Shelburne, MA   Franklin County

See Driving Directions, What to Expect,
and Trail Information.

Late Season

Dirt road trail off parking lot and past iron bar: Common
Blackberry (beginning to bloom), Robin's Plantain, Common
Cinquefoil, Buttercup (beginning to bloom), Strawberry, Wild
Columbine, Canada Mayflower [Wild Lily-of-the-valley],
Starflower, False Solomon's Seal [Wild Spikenard]

Turn right at first Lady's Slipper Trail sign;   Canada
Mayflower [Wild Lily-of-the-valley], False Solomon's Seal
[Wild Spikenard] (buds), Foamflower [False Miterwort] (near
end of bloom), Hairy Solomon's Seal (look under the leaves),
Canada Mayflower [Wild Lily-of-the-valley], Common
Cinquefoil, Maple-leaved Viburnum [Dockmackie] (buds),
Pink Lady's Slipper [Moccasin Flower], Pink Azalea [Pinxter
Flower] (near end of bloom - most ended)

Middle of June

The Norcross Wildlife Sanctuary at Tupper Hill

Monson and Wales, MA   Hampden County

See Driving Directions, What to Expect,
and Trail Information.

Early Season

Entrance area: Canada Hawkweed, Highbush Cranberry (near end of bloom), Jack-in-the-pulpit [Indian Turnip], Rhododendron, Orange Hawkweed [Devil's Paintbrush]

Start by leaving the Visitors Center from the left side door. Follow sidewalk and then turn right: Gray Beardtongue, Wild Columbine, Canada Hawkweed, Oxeye Daisy, Field Hawkweed [King Devil], Common Cinquefoil

Turn left into Hickory Grove at sign for Short Trail: Bluets [Quaker Ladies, Innocence], Field Hawkweed [Devil's Paintbrush], Yellow Stargrass, Robin's Plantain (near end of bloom), Common Cinquefoil, Common Speedwell

Through gate to fenced-in area of Short Trail: Wild Geranium [Spotted Cranesbill], Jack-in-the-pulpit [Indian Turnip] (near end of bloom), False Solomon's Seal [Wild Spikenard], Wild Columbine, Bluestar, Azalea (orange), Fire Pink, Fly Poison, Heart-leaved Alexanders, Fairy Wand [Devil's Bit, Blazing Star], Eared Coreopsis, Ragwort, Rose Trillium, Wild Bleeding Heart, Common Blackberry, Green Trillium, Golden Alexanders, Dog Hobble, Creeping Phlox (near end of bloom), Smaller Yellow Lady's Slipper

Gate out of Short Trail, across road and into Conifer Grove: Bluets [Quaker Ladies, Innocence], Field Hawkweed [King Devil], Robin's Plantain, Oxeye Daisy, Common Cinquefoil, Common Speedwell, Yellow Stargrass, Golden Ragwort, False [White] Hellebore [Indian Poke]

Into Upland Shrub area: Wild Geranium [Spotted Cranesbill], Bluets [Quaker Ladies, Innocence], Starflower [May Star]

Go out of Upland Shrub area and turn left to continue along path. Turn right to skip Upper Trail. Bear left toward Boardwalk, Lime Cobbles, and Pine Barren Garden. Turn right onto the Boardwalk.: False [White] Hellebore [Indian Poke], Ragwort

Go right at Pond Trail: Larger Blue Flag Iris [Blue Flag Iris] (one), Common Cinquefoil, Bluets [Quaker Ladies, Innocence], Common Speedwell

Go right at pond and follow path around it: Yarrow [Milfoil], Common Blackberry, Larger Blue Flag Iris [Blue Flag Iris], Wild Lupine (quite a few), Oxeye Daisy, Hairy Beardtongue (many), Bluestar, Poppy Mallow, Albino Blue Flag Iris, Field Hawkweed [King Devil], White [Foxglove] Beardtongue, Yellow Iris, Wild Columbine

Leave pond area by turning right. Follow Boardwalk to right and turn right at Circle Garden: Wild Geranium [Spotted Cranesbill], Starflower [May Star], Showy Skullcap, Buttercup, False [White] Hellebore [Indian Poke], Golden Ragwort, Jack-in-the-pulpit [Indian Turnip] (near end of bloom), Larger Blue Flag Iris [Blue Flag Iris], Field Hawkweed [King Devil], Water [Purple] Avens (near end of bloom), Canada Mayflower [Wild Lily-of-the-valley]

Cross bridge: Large-flowered Trillium [Great White Trillium], Red Baneberry

Go to left at Lime Flower Cobble: Wild Geranium [Spotted Cranesbill], Golden Ragwort (near end of bloom), Wild Columbine, Wild Blue Phlox, Golden Alexanders, Robin's Plantain, Rue Anemone, Fire Pink, Foamflower [False Miterwort] (near end of bloom), Greek Valerian, Smaller

Yellow Lady's Slipper, Shooting Star (white), Golden Star, Oxeye Daisy, Wild Bleeding Heart, Virginia Waterleaf (white), Blue-eyed Grass

Go up the steps to the field: Bluets [Quaker Ladies, Innocence], Field Hawkweed [King Devil], Robin's Plantain, Yarrow [Milfoil], Buttercup, Blue-eyed Grass

Go left at field and then right around edge of field: Same flowers as those observed going up the steps plus Maiden Pink (many in places), Oxeye Daisy, Common Cinquefoil, Sheep Laurel [Lambkill]

Turn left into the Pine Barren area: Yarrow [Milfoil], Bluets [Quaker Ladies, Innocence], Common Cinquefoil, Blue-eyed Grass, Turkey Beard, Sheep Laurel [Lambkill] (beginning to bloom), Pitcher Plant, Buttercup

Right at Holly Circle: Holly

Go back to Lower Trail and take bridge left to Visitors Center.

Chapelbrook Falls

Chapelbrook Reservation
South Ashfield, MA   Franklin County

See Driving Directions, What to Expect,
and Trail Information.

Late Season

Along the road into the reservation (going downhill) - stop at large rocks: Buttercup, False Solomon's Seal [Wild Spikenard], Canada Mayflower [Wild Lily-of-the-valley] (near end of bloom)

Mount Sugarloaf State Reservation

South Deerfield, MA   Franklin County

See Driving Directions, What to Expect,
and Trail Information.

Late Season

Trail from lower parking lot. Smaller Pussytoes (beginning to bloom), Robin's Plantain (near end of bloom), Field Hawkweed [King Devil] (beginning to bloom), Common Cinquefoil (many), Swamp Dewberry, Strawberry, White Campion, Rough Cinquefoil, Daisy Fleabane [Sweet Scabious], Bluets [Quaker Ladies, Innocence], Yellow Wood Sorrel, False Solomon's Seal [Wild Spikenard]

Into woods: Maple-leaved Viburnum [Dockmackie] (near end of bloom), Jack-in-the-pulpit [Indian Turnip] (near end of bloom)

Power line area: Wild Geranium [Spotted Cranesbill] (quite a few), Thimbleweed [Tall Anemone]

Continue bearing right: Mountain Laurel (a bit of bloom), Bush Honeysuckle (one)

Turned around at sign for summit.

Sanderson Brook Falls

Chester-Blandford State Forest
Chester and Blandford, MA   Hampden County

See Driving Directions, What to Expect,
and Trail Information.

Late Season

Sanderson Brook Road toward the falls: False Solomon's Seal [Wild Spikenard] (few), Golden Alexanders (few), Common Blackberry, Jack-in-the-pulpit [Indian Turnip] (quite a few), Common Cinquefoil, Strawberry (near end of bloom), Violet (medium purple - few), Wood Nettle (beginning to bloom - many plants), Canada Mayflower [Wild Lily-of-the-valley] (few), White Baneberry [Doll's Eyes] (few), Violet (white), Sweet Cicely (two), Virginia Waterleaf (most white, a few purple), Hairy Solomon's Seal (few - look under the leaves), Foamflower [False Miterwort] (near end of bloom), Bluets [Quaker Ladies, Innocence], Striped Maple tree

Turn right at blue arrow to path down to waterfalls and area near waterfalls: Violet (purple, medium purple), Strawberry (quite a few), Jack-in-the-pulpit [Indian Turnip], Golden Alexanders (few), Wild Sarsaparilla (few - near end of bloom), Common Winter Cress [Yellow Rocket] (quite a few), Foamflower [False Miterwort] (few)

Cascade Falls

North Adams, MA   Berkshire County

See Driving Directions, What to Expect, and Trail Information.

Late Season

Trail to Cascade Falls: Yellow Avens (quite a few), Common Blackberry, Buttercup, Maple-leaved Viburnum [Dockmackie], Bush Honeysuckle, Sweet-scented Bedstraw, Virginia Waterleaf (white and light purple), Round-leaved

Ragwort (near end of bloom), Shinleaf (buds), Starflower (finished), Common Cinquefoil

Over bridge and continue on trail: Trillium (gone to seed), Hairy Solomon's Seal (leaves), Canada Mayflower [Wild Lily-of-the-valley], Indian Cucumber Root (look under the leaves - one), False Solomon's Seal (berries beginning), Yellow Clintonia [Bluebead] (berries beginning)

Walk along the edge of the stream a short way: Wood Nettle

Over a tiny stream: Robin's Plantain (one), Golden Alexanders (few - near end of bloom), Tall Meadow Rue (one), Smaller Forget-me-not (few), Foamflower [False Miterwort] (near end of bloom), Jack-in-the-pulpit [Indian Turnip] (most near end of bloom)

End of June

The Norcross Wildlife Sanctuary at Tupper Hill

Monson and Wales, MA   Hampden County

See Driving Directions, What to Expect,
and Trail Information.

Late Season

Entrance area: Canada Hawkweed, Ground Ivy [Gill-over-the-ground], Multiflora Rose, Field Hawkweed [King Devil], Oxeye Daisy, Buttercup, Cow [Tufted] Vetch

Start by leaving the Visitors Center from the left side door. After the sidewalk turn right and then turn left toward the Short Trail: Field Hawkweed [King Devil], Oxeye Daisy, Bluets [Quaker Ladies, Innocence], Panicled Hawkweed, Yellow Stargrass, Wild Columbine (one), Dwarf Cinquefoil

Through gate to fenced-in area of Short Trail: Wild Geranium [Spotted Cranesbill] (near end of bloom), White [Foxglove] Beardtongue, Ozark Phlox [Downy Phlox], Fire Pink, Bush Honeysuckle, Bushpea (beginning to bloom), Wild Bleeding Heart (near end of bloom), Flame Azalea, Pale [Pink] Corydalis, Golden Alexanders, Turkey Beard, Fly Poison, Eared Coreopsis, Mountain Phlox, Bowman's Root [Indian Physic], Creeping Phlox (near end of bloom), Foamflower [False Miterwort] (near end of bloom), Alumroot

Gate out of wildflower garden (Short Trail), through Conifer Grove, Lower Trail, and right onto Boardwalk: Smaller Purple Fringed Orchis

Pond Trail: Bluets [Quaker Ladies, Innocence], Common Cinquefoil, Yellow Iris, Slender Blue Flag Iris (near end of bloom), Hairy Beardtongue, Spotted Monkey Flower, Bluestar, Common Blackberry (near end of bloom), Fly Poison, Yarrow [Milfoil], Oxeye Daisy, White [Foxglove] Beardtongue, Rough-fruited [Sulphur] Cinquefoil, Poppy Mallow, Wild Lupine

Mount Greylock State Reservation

Cheshire and New Ashford, MA   Berkshire County

See Driving Directions, What to Expect,
and Trail Information.

Early Season

Jones Nose Trail through field: Buttercup, Common Cinquefoil (many), Strawberry, Orange Hawkweed [Devil's Paintbrush] (quite a few), Blue-eyed Grass (quite a few), Yarrow [Milfoil] (beginning to bloom), Thimbleberry [Black Raspberry], One-flowered Cancerroot [Ghost Pipe], Common Blackberry (many), Maiden Pink (beginning to bloom), Naked Withrod [Possum Haw]

Jones Nose Trail and CCC Dynamite Trail in woods: Common Cinquefoil, Common Blackberry (beginning to bloom), Sweet Cicely (near end of bloom), Virginia Waterleaf (white, lavender), Common Wood Sorrel (many in places), Canada Mayflower [Wild Lily-of-the-valley], Jack-in-the-pulpit [Indian Turnip], Violet (white with yellow center and purple lines in the center), Foamflower [False Miterwort] (near end of bloom), Yellow Clintonia [Bluebead] (near end of bloom)

Turned around at a small stream with a rock to cross it and a very small waterfall on the right.

High Ledges Wildlife Sanctuary

Shelburne, MA   Franklin County

See Driving Directions, What to Expect, and Trail Information.

Late Season

<u>By main parking area</u>: Meadowsweet (beginning to bloom), Field Hawkweed [King Devil] (near end of bloom), Buttercup, Common Cinquefoil

<u>Down road toward entrance (not past metal bar)</u>: Red Clover (many), Yarrow [Milfoil], Field Hawkweed [King Devil], Buttercup, Whorled [Four-leaved] Loosestrife (many), Bush Honeysuckle, Common Cinquefoil, Common Blackberry (near end of bloom), Blue-eyed Grass (one), Sheep Laurel [Lambkill] (many in one place), Orange Hawkweed [Devil's Paintbrush]

<u>Left on Waterthrush Trail</u>: Common Blackberry (near end of bloom), Orange Hawkweed [Devil's Paintbrush], Mountain Laurel, Whorled [Four-leaved] Loosestrife, Common Cinquefoil

<u>Into woods on trail for a short distance</u>: Mountain Laurel (many - beginning to bloom)

<u>Trail straight behind main parking area</u>: Common Cinquefoil, Field Hawkweed [King Devil] (near end of bloom), Lesser Stitchwort, Yarrow [Milfoil], Maiden Pink (many in one area), Orange Hawkweed [Devil's Paintbrush] (near end of bloom)

<u>Stop at stone wall at the edge of the woods</u>.

Gunn Brook Falls

Sunderland, MA   Franklin County

See Driving Directions, What to Expect,
and Trail Information.

Late Season

Wildflower plants near short unmarked trail to the bottom of the falls: False Solomon's Seal [Wild Spikenard] (finished and forming berries), Jack-in-the-pulpit [Indian Turnip] (finished), Wake-robin [Birthroot, Purple or Red Trillium] (finished)

Slatestone Brook Falls

Sunderland, MA   Franklin County

See Driving Directions, What to Expect,
and Trail Information.

Late Season

Flowers below falls: Smaller Forget-me-not

Flowers on other side of the bridge: Celandine, Motherwort, Multiflora Rose

Beginning of July

The Norcross Wildlife Sanctuary at Tupper Hill

Monson and Wales, MA   Hampden County

See Driving Directions, What to Expect,
and Trail Information.

Late Season

Entrance area: Fall Dandelion

Start by leaving the Visitors Center from the left side door.
After the sidewalk turn right and then turn left toward the
Short Trail: Oxeye Daisy, Yarrow [Milfoil], Yellow Stargrass

Through gate to fenced-in area of Short Trail: Black
Snakeroot [Black Cohosh] (beginning to bloom), Ozark
[Downy] Phlox, Gray Beardtongue, Sundrops, Wild Quinine
[American Feverfew] (beginning to bloom), Bush
Honeysuckle,, Bushpea Caroliniana, Wild Bleeding Heart
(near end of bloom), Pale [Pink] Corydalis, Kousa [Japanese,
Korean] Dogwood, Wild Columbine (near end of bloom), Fly
Poison (green), Turk's-cap Lily, Harebell [Bluebell], Indian
Pink,   Mountain Phlox, Bowman's Root [Indian Physic],
Goatsbeard, Climbing Fumitory [Mountain Fringe or
Allegheny Vine], Wild Hydrangea (beginning to bloom), Tall
Meadow Rue, Enchanter's Nightshade

Gate out of wildflower garden (Short Trail), across road, and
through Conifer Grove to Lower Trail: Black-eyed Susan

Lower Trail to Boardwalk - then turn right onto Boardwalk:
Smaller Purple Fringed Orchis

Trail to pond and right around pond: Whorled [Four-leaved]
Loosestrife, Yarrow [Milfoil], Bluets [Quaker Ladies,
Innocence], Dewberry, Heather [Ling], Oxeye Daisy, Field
Hawkweed [King Devil], Daisy Fleabane [Sweet Scabious],
Lesser Daisy Fleabane, Wild Lupine, Sundrops, Common St.
Johnswort, Gray Beardtongue, Rough-fruited [Sulphur]
Cinquefoil, Butterfly Weed [Pleurisy Root], Poppy Mallow,
Prickly Pear Cactus, Small Sundrops, Heart-leaved Skullcap,
Poppy Mallow (other type), Spotted Monkey Flower

Out of pond area, to right on Boardwalk and up steps to field.
Turn left along edge of field and then right to continue along
edge. Find Pine Barren sign: Some flowers seen before plus
Colicroot

Path through Pine Barren: Grass Pink [Grass Pink Orchid],
Sticky Tofieldia, Common St. Johnswort (beginning to
bloom), Smooth Azalea (near end of bloom), Shrubby
Cinquefoil, Meadowsweet, Swamp Candles [Yellow
Loosestrife], Swamp Milkweed, Staggerbush

Cedar Swamp to Meadow Garden: Orange Hawkweed
[Devil's Paintbrush], Yarrow [Milfoil], Cow [Tufted] Vetch,
Wild Bergamot (large), Sundrops, Black-eyed Susan, Yellow
Stargrass, Common Milkweed

Go back to Lower Trail and take bridge left to Visitors Center.

Mount Greylock State Reservation

Cheshire and New Ashford, MA   Berkshire County

See Driving Directions, What to Expect,
and Trail Information.

Early Season

Jones Nose Trail through field: White Avens, Common
Cinquefoil, Buttercup, Common Speedwell, Meadowsweet
(beginning to bloom), Yarrow [Milfoil], Selfheal [Heal-all],
Maiden Pink, Orange Hawkweed [Devil's Paintbrush],
Fireweed [Great Willow Herb] (beginning to bloom),
Common Blackberry, Dewberry, Field Hawkweed [King
Devil] (near end of bloom)

Jones Nose Trail and CCC Dynamite Trail in woods: Common Cinquefoil, Field Hawkweed [King Devil], White Avens, Bush Honeysuckle, Common Wood Sorrel, False [White] Hellebore [Indian Poke], Daisy Fleabane [Sweet Scabious] (one), Wild Leek [Ramps] (beginning to bloom), Jack-in-the-pulpit [Indian Turnip], Wood Nettle, Virginia Waterleaf (near end of bloom), Tall Meadow Rue

Turned around at a tiny stream with a waterfall on the right. The waterfall was now down to a trickle.

High Ledges Wildlife Sanctuary

Shelburne, MA   Franklin County

See Driving Directions, What to Expect,
and Trail Information.

Early Season

Field before parking lot and gate: Steeplebush [Hardhack], Yarrow [Milfoil], Purple Milkweed, Buttercup, Common Milkweed, Red Clover, Common St. Johnswort, Whorled [Four-leaved] Loosestrife, Bush Honeysuckle, Wood Lily, Canada Lily [Meadow Lily, Wild Yellow Lily], Swamp Dewberry, Sheep Laurel [Lambkill]

Dirt road past iron bar gate: Common Milkweed, Buttercup, Steeplebush [Hardhack], Yarrow [Milfoil], Bush Honeysuckle, Red Clover, Whorled [Four-leaved] Loosestrife, Selfheal [Heal-all], Dewberry, Shinleaf, Common Blackberry, Lesser Stitchwort, Yellow Wood Sorrel, Daisy Fleabane [Sweet Scabious], Cowwheat, Swamp Dewberry, Mountain Laurel (near end of bloom), Single Pink Rose, Pale [Pink] Corydalis

Go right at second Lady's Slipper Trail sign (past cabin) and follow trail markers: Cowwheat (many)

Bear left at the second sign for Wolves Den Trail. Go straight at Gentian Swamp: Pitcher Plant, Blue Flag Iris, Swamp Dewberry, Small Cranberry, Shrubby Cinquefoil, Yarrow [Milfoil], Mountain Laurel (near end of bloom), Small Sundrops

Stop at end of swamp and boardwalk, go back to Lady's Slipper Trail and turn left onto Lady's Slipper Trail. Dwarf Ginseng, Indian Cucumber Root, Mountain Laurel (near end of bloom), Canada Lily [Meadow Lily, Wild Yellow Lily], Purple-flowering Raspberry

Cross stream and turn left. Trail signs change to yellow indicating that you are going back toward the parking lot. Continue following the yellow markers back to the dirt road and then turn left toward the parking lot.

Middle of July

Mount Greylock State Reservation

New Ashford and Cheshire, MA   Berkshire County

See Driving Directions, What to Expect,
and Trail Information.

Early Season

Jones Nose Trail - meadow: Maiden Pink (quite a few), Daisy Fleabane [Sweet Scabious], Buttercup, Selfheal [Heal-all], Meadowsweet (light pink and creamy white - many), White

Avens (near end of bloom), Common St. Johnswort, Yarrow [Milfoil] (quite a few), Common Mullein, Fireweed [Great Willow Herb] (many), Common Milkweed, Steeplebush [Hardhack] (beginning to bloom), Orange Hawkweed [Devil's Paintbrush] (few), Common Evening Primrose

Trail into woods: Yarrow [Milfoil], Pale Touch-me-not [Jewelweed] (beginning to bloom), Tall Meadow Rue (near end of bloom), Daisy Fleabane [Sweet Scabious], Common Wood Sorrel (two), Wild Leek [Ramps] (many)

Left on CCC Dynamite trail: Flower not seen before - Wood Nettle

Turned around at a small stream with a rock to cross it. The tiny waterfall to the right is almost silent.

The Norcross Wildlife Sanctuary at Tupper Hill

Monson and Wales, MA   Hampden County

See Driving Directions, What to Expect,
and Trail Information.

Late Season

Start by leaving the Visitors Center from the left side door. Garden to the right: Great Beardtongue, Wild Columbine

Turn right and then left into the Hickory Grove towards the Short Trail: Indian Pipe [Corpse Plant], Yellow Stargrass, Oxeye Daisy (few - near end of bloom)

Through the gate to fenced-in area of the Short Trail: Black Snakeroot [Black Cohosh] (many), Cup Plant [Indian Cup],

Helleborine, Sundrops, Turk's-cap Lily (near end of bloom), Great Beardtongue (one), Mountain Phlox, Wild Hydrangea, Wild Bleeding Heart (near end of bloom), Nodding Wild Onion (pink), Climbing Hydrangea, Harebell [Bluebell], Tall Meadow Rue (near end of bloom)

Gate out of wildflower garden (Short Trail), across road, through Conifer Grove to Acid Rock Garden: Harebell [Bluebell]

Skip Upland Shrubs, cross a stream, and take a right toward the Lower Trail. Bear left toward the boardwalk to the pond. Follow signs to the pond and go right around the pond.: Yarrow [Milfoil], Common St. Johnswort, Daisy Fleabane [Sweet Scabious], Blue Toadflax, Great Beardtongue, Hairy Beardtongue, Butterfly Weed [Pleurisy Root], Poppy Mallow, Swamp Milkweed, Scarlet Monkey Flower, Oxeye Daisy, Cape Golden [Sickle-leaved Golden] Aster, Upland Aster [Upland White Aster], Spotted Monkey Flower, Cardinal Flower, Fly Poison

Back to boardwalk, continue right on boardwalk, and then right into the Circle Garden: Swamp Milkweed, Hairy Wood Mint

Up steps to field: Black Snakeroot [Black Cohosh], Hairy Wood Mint

Turn left to follow the edge of the field. Turn right to continue around the edge of the field.: Colicroot, Bladder Campion, Black-eyed Susan, Maiden Pink, Rough-fruited [Sulphur] Cinquefoil

Go left into the Pine Barren area: Dewberry, Common St. Johnswort (near end of bloom), Clammy Azalea [Swamp

Honeysuckle] (near end of bloom), Steeplebush [Hardhack] (beginning to bloom), Swamp Milkweed

Go back onto Lower Trail and take bridge left to Visitors Center.

Beginning of August

Mount Sugarloaf State Reservation

South Deerfield, MA   Franklin County

See Driving Directions, What to Expect,
and Trail Information.

Late Season

Trail from lower parking lot: Daisy Fleabane [Sweet Scabious], Selfheal [Heal-all], Red Clover, Spiked Lobelia, Lady's Thumb, Yellow Wood Sorrel, White Avens, Spotted St. Johnswort, White Campion, Enchanter's Nightshade (near end of bloom), Common Burdock, Pokeweed

Turned around after the open area.

High Ledges Wildlife Sanctuary

Shelburne, MA   Franklin County

See Driving Directions, What to Expect,
and Trail Information.

Late Season

<u>Beside parking lot</u>:   Goldenrod, Common St. Johnswort, Silvery Cinquefoil, Common Milkweed (near end of bloom), Red Clover, Yarrow [Milfoil], Purple Milkweed

<u>Road toward entrance (not past iron bar)</u>:   Some flowers mentioned before plus Steeplebush [Hardhack], Selfheal [Heal-all]

Gunn Brook Falls

Sunderland, MA   Franklin County

See Driving Directions, What to Expect,
and Trail Information.

Late Season

<u>Wildflower plants along the short path toward the bottom of falls</u>:   False Solomon's Seal [Wild Spikenard] (berries), Trillium (flowers finished), Aster (leaves), Jack-in-the-pulpit [Indian Turnip] (leaves only)

Slatestone Brook Falls

Sunderland, MA   Franklin County

See Driving Directions, What to Expect,
and Trail Information.

Late Season

Flowers by the falls: Pale Touch-me-not [Jewelweed],
Spotted Touch-me-not [Jewelweed], Pokeweed, Lady's
Thumb, Yellow Wood Sorrel, Tall Nettle, Common Burdock

Mount Greylock State Reservation

New Ashford and Cheshire, MA   Berkshire County

See Driving Directions, What to Expect,
and Trail Information.

Late Season

Jones Nose Trail (meadow): Maiden Pink, Yarrow [Milfoil]
(few), Buttercup, Meadowsweet (many), Purple-stemmed
Aster, White Snakeroot, Wild Basil, Enchanter's Nightshade,
Fireweed [Great Willow Herb] (many), Butter-and-eggs
(few), Agrimony, Steeplebush [Hardhack] (many), Goldenrod
(beginning to bloom), Common St. Johnswort (few), Orange
Hawkweed [Devil's Paintbrush] (few), Canada Hawkweed
(one), Common Evening Primrose

Jones Nose Trail in Woods: Pale Touch-me-not [Jewelweed],
White Snakeroot (barely beginning), Sharp-leaved [Mountain,
Whorled] Aster, Zigzag [Broad-leaved] Goldenrod

Turn around when trail divides - Dynamite Trail left and
Summit Trail right.

Wildflower Photographs for Identification

Irregular Flowers

Basal Leaves Only

1A Pink Lady's Slipper (x1/2)
[Moccasin Flower]

1B Grass Pink (x1/3)
[Grass Pink Orchid]

1C Shooting Star (x1/3)

1D Jack-in-the-pulpit (x1/3)
[Indian Turnip]
(also green and white)

1E Dutchman's Breeches (x1/2)

1F Squirrel Corn (x1/2)

Irregular Flowers

Alternate Leaves

2A Spiked Lobelia
(x1)

2B White Sweet Clover
(x1/10)

2C Butter-and-eggs
(x1/2)

2E Birdsfoot Trefoil
(x2/3)

2D Great Lobelia
(x2/5)

2F Red Clover
(x2/5)

2G Wood Betony
(x1/2) [Lousewort]

Irregular Flowers

Alternate Leaves

3A Wild Lupine (x1/2)

3B Yellow Fringed Orchis (x1/2)
[Yellow Fringed Orchid]

3C Pale or Pink Corydalis
(x3/4)

3D Wild Monkshood (x1/2)

Alternate Leaves

4A Cardinal Flower (x1/4)

4B Fringed Polygala (x2/3)
[Flowering Wintergreen or Gaywings]

4C Crown Vetch (x2/3)
[Axseed]

4D Pale Touch-me-not (x1)
[Jewelweed]

4E Spotted Touch-me-not (x1)
[Jewelweed]

Irregular Flowers

Alternate Leaves

5A Larger Yellow Lady's Slipper
(x2/3)

5B Viper's Bugloss (x1)
[Blueweed]

Opposite Leaves

5C Selfheal (x1)
[Heal-all]

5D Horse Balm (x1/2)
[Richweed or Stoneroot]

5E Turtlehead (x2/5)

5F Common Speedwell (x1)

Opposite Leaves

6A White [Foxglove] Beardtongue (x2/5)

6B Scarlet Monkey Flower (x2/3)

6C Dittany (x1/2)

6D Downy Skullcap (x1/2)

6E Narrow-leaved Mountain Mint (x1/2)

6F Ground Ivy (x1) [Gill-over-the-ground]

Irregular Flowers

Opposite Leaves

7A Horsemint (x1/5)
[Dotted Horsemint]

7B Wild Basil (x1/2)

7C Motherwort (x1)

7D Wild Bergamot (x2/5)

Vines

7E Hog Peanut (x1/2)

7F Cow [Tufted] Vetch (x1/2)

Flowers with Three Regular Parts

Basal Leaves

8A Wild Ginger (x2/3)

Alternate Leaves

8B Crested Iris (x1/2)
[Dwarf Crested Iris]

8C Larger Blue Flag Iris (x1/3)

8D Yellow Iris (x1/4)

Whorled Leaves

8E Prairie Trillium (x3/4)

8F Toad Trillium (x3/4)
[Toadshade] (also green)

Flowers with Three Regular Parts

Whorled Leaves

9A Large-flowered [White] Trillium (x3/4)

9C Rose Trillium (x3/4)

9B Wake-robin
[Birthroot or Purple or Red Trillium]
(x3/4)

10A Dame's Violet (x1/2)
[Dame's Rocket]
(also light purple or white)

10B Canada Mayflower (x1/2)
[Wild Lily-of-the-valley]

10C Garlic Mustard (x2/3)

10D Cuckooflower (x1/2)
[Lady's Smock]

10E Fireweed (x3/4)
[Great Willow Herb]

10F Common Evening Primrose (x1/2)

Flowers with Four Regular Parts

Alternate Leaves

11A Early Meadow Rue (x1/2)

11B Tall Meadow Rue (x1/2)

11C Celandine (x3/4)

Opposite Leaves

11D Toothwort (x1/2)
[Crinkleroot]

11E Fringed Gentian (x1/2)

11F Bluets (x2/3)
[Quaker Ladies or Innocence]

Flowers with Four and Five Regular Parts

Four Regular Parts - Shrub

12A Panicled [Gray]
Dogwood (x1/2)

12B Flowering Dogwood (x1/2)

12C Virgin's Bower (x1/2)

Five Regular Parts -
No Apparent Leaves at
Flowering Time

12D Heather (x1/2) [Ling]

Five Regular Parts -
Basal Leaves Only

12E Indian Pipe (x1/3)
[Corpse Plant]

12F Common Wood Sorrell
(x1/2)

Flowers with Five Regular Parts

Basal Leaves Only

13A Early Saxifrage (x1/2)

13B Pitcher Plant (x1/2)

13C Foamflower (x1/2)
[False Miterwort]

13D Wild Sarsaparilla (x1/2)

Alternate Leaves

13E Yellow Wood
Sorrel (x1/2)

13F Virginia Waterleaf
(x1/2)

13G Smaller
Forget-me-not (x1)

Flowers with Five Regular Parts

Alternate Leaves

14A Silvery
Cinquefoil (x1)

14B Rough
Cinquefoil (x1)

14C Common
Cinquefoil (x1)

14D Rough-fruited
[Sulphur] Cinquefoil
(x1)

14E Wild Carrot (x1/2)
[Queen Ann's Lace,
Bird's Nest]

14F Yarrow (x1/2)
[Milfoil]

14G Poppy Mallow
(x1/2)

14H
Water Smartweed
(x1/2)

14I Spotted Knapweed
(x1/2)

Flowers with Five Regular Parts

Alternate Leaves

15A Common Blackberry
(x1/2)

15B Marsh Marigold (x1/2)
[Cowslip]

15C Wild Columbine (x1/2)

15D Blue Flax (x1/2)

15E Butterfly Weed (x1/2)
[Pleurisy Root]

15F Virginia Bluebells (x1/2)
[Virginia Cowslip]

Alternate Leaves

16A Harebell (x1/2) [Bluebell]

16B Agrimony (x3/4)

16C Wild Parsnip (x1/2)

16D Common Mullein (x1/2)

16E Grass-of-Parnassus
(x3/4)

Opposite or Whorled Leaves

16F Herb Robert (x1)

Flowers with Five Regular Parts

Opposite or Whorled Leaves

17A Wild Geranium (x1/2)
[Spotted Cranesbill]

17B Swamp Milkweed (x1/2)
(pink to rose-purple)

17C Whorled
[Four-leaved]
Loosestrife (x1/2)

17D Wood Anemone (x1/2)
[Windflower]

17E Fringed Loosestrife (x1/2)

17F Swamp Candles (x1/2)
[Yellow Loosestrife]

Flowers with Five Regular Parts

Opposite or Whorled Leaves

18A Dwarf Ginseng (x1)

18B Thimbleweed (x1/2)
[Tall Anemone]

Opposite Leaves

18C Ragged Robin (x1/2)
[Cuckooflower]

18D Carolina Spring Beauty
(x1/2)

18E Blue Vervain (x1/2)

18F Miterwort (x2)
[Bishop's Cap]

Flowers with Five Regular Parts

Opposite Leaves

19A Bladder Campion (x1/2)
(bladder sometimes green
or beige)

19B White Campion (x1/2)

19C Bouncing Bet (x1/2)
[Soapwort] (also pink)

19D Spreading Dogbane (x1/2)

19E Fine-barren Gentian
(x1/2)

19F Closed Gentian (x1/2)
[Bottle Gentian]

Flowers with Five Regular Parts

Opposite Leaves

20A Maiden Pink (x2/3)

20B Deptford Pink (x2/3)

20C Spotted St. Johnswort (x2/3)

20D Smooth False Foxglove (x1/2)

20E Common St. Johnswort (x1/2)

Shrubs

20F Shrubby Cinquefoil (x1/2)

20G Mountain Laurel (x1/2)

20H Purple-flowering Raspberry (x1/2)

Flowers with Five Regular Parts

Shrubs

21A Maple-leaved Viburnum
(x1/2) [Dockmackie]

21B Shadbush (x1/2)
[Smooth or Common Shadbush]

21C Steeplebush (x1/2)
[Hardhack]

21D Meadowsweet (x1/2)

Shrubs

22A Common Elder (x2/5)

22B Chokecherry
(x1/2)

22C Wild Hydrangea (x1/2)

22D Multiflora Rose (x1/2)

Flowers with Five Regular Parts

Shrubs

23A Rugosa Rose (x2/5)

23B Pink Azalea (x1/2)
[Pinxter Flower]

Shrubs

24A Morrow's Honeysuckle (x1/2)

24B Tartarian Honeysuckle (x1/2)

24C Hybrid of Morrow's and Tartarian Honeysuckle (x1/2)

24D Hobblebush (x1/2)

Vines

25B Swamp Dewberry (x1/2)
(Dewberry similar but larger)

25A Hedge Bindweed (x1/2)

25C Bittersweet Nightshade
(x1/2)

25D Trumpet [Coral] Honeysuckle (x1/2)

Flowers with Six Regular Parts

Basal Leaves Only

26A Yellow Stargrass (x1/2)

26B Blue-eyed Grass (x1)

26C Yellow Clintonia (x1/2)
[Bluebead]

26D Trout Lily (x1/2)
[Yellow Adder's Tongue]

26E Swamp Pink (x1/2)
[Swamp Hyacinth]

26F Colicroot (x1/2)

Alternate Leaves

27A Sessile-leaved Bellwort (x1/2) [Wild Oats]

27B False [White] Hellibore (x1/2) [Wild Spikenard]

27C Hairy Solomon's Seal (x1/2)

27D Turkey Beard (x1/2)

27E False Solomon's Seal (x2/5)
[Wild Spikenard]

Flowers with Six Regular Parts

Opposite or Whorled Leaves

28A Mayapple (x1/2)
[Mandrake]

28B Purple Loosestrife (x1/2)

28C Indian Cucumber Root (x1/2)

28D Blue Cohosh (x1/2)
(also purplish)

28E Turk's-cap Lily (x1/2)

28F Canada Lily (x1/2)
[Meadow Lily or Wild Yellow
Lily] (also yellow or red)

Flowers with Six or Seven Regular Parts

Vine with Six Regular Parts

29A Wild Balsam Apple (1/4)
[Wild Cucumber]

Seven or More Regular Parts. No Leaves at Flowering Time.

29B Coltsfoot (x1/2)

Seven or More Regular Parts - Basal Leaves

29C Bloodroot (X1/2)

29D Orange Hawkweed (x1/2)
[Devil's Paintbrush]

29E Field Hawkweed (x1/2) [King Devil]

29F Mouse Ear (x1/2)

Flowers with Seven or More Regular Parts

Whorled Leaves

30A Round-lobed Hepatica (x1/2)
[Liverleaf] (also blue, violet
and white)

Alternate Leaves

30B Ragwort (x1/2)
(Golden or Round-leaved)

30C Nipplewort (x1/2)

30D Yellow Goatsbeard (x1/2)

30E Sneezeweed (x1/2)

30F Chicory (x1/2)

30G Daisy Fleabane (x1/2)
[Sweet Scabious]

Flowers with Seven or More Regular Parts

Alternate Leaves

31A Blanket Flower (x1/2)

31B Oxeye Daisy (x1/2)

31C Tall [Green Headed] Coneflower (x1/2)

31D Robin's Plantain (x1/2)

31E Black-eyed Susan (x1/2)

Seven or More Regular Parts

32A Starflower (x1/2)
[May Star]

32B Rue Anemone (x1/2)

32C Cup Plant (x1/3)
[Indian Cup]

Parts Indistinguishable - Alternate Leaves

32D White Baneberry (x1/2)
[Doll's Eyes]

32E Common Burdock (x1/2)

32F Golden Alexanders (x1/2)

Alternate Leaves

33A Black Snakeroot (x1/4)
[Black Cohosh]

33B Canada Thistle (x1/2)

33C Wood Nettle (x1/2)

Flowers with Parts Indistinguishable

Alternate Leaves

34A Spiked Blazing Star (x2/5)
[Dense Blazing Star]

Opposite or Whorled Leaves

34B Boneset (x1/3)
[Thoroughwort]

34C White Snakeroot (x1/3)

34D Spotted Joe-Pye Weed (x1/3)

Flowers with Parts Indistinguishable

Opposite Leaves

35A Tall Nettle (x1/3)

Goldenrods

35C Silverod (x2/5)

35B Zigzag Goldenrod (x2/5)
[Broad-leaved Goldenrod]

35D Blue-stemmed Goldenrod (x2/5)
[Wreath Goldenrod]

Heart-shaped Leaves
Basal Leaves Less Than 3 Inches Wide or None

36A White Wood Aster (x2/5)
[Wood Aster]

36B Heart-leaved Aster (x2/5)
(light blue-violet, light rose,
or white)

36C Lowrie's Aster (x 2/5)
(stem to leaf is winged; flowers
pale blue, blue, or pinkish)

Basal Leaves 3 in. Wide
or More

36E Large-leaved Aster (x2/5)
(violet or lavender)

36D Schreber's Aster (x2/5)

Leaves not Heart-shaped

37A Heath Aster (x2/5)
(uppermost leaves
sharply pointed)

37B Panicled Aster (x2/5)
(leaves narrowly lance-shaped;
flower heads 3/4-1 in. wide;
white or tinged with violet)

37C Flat-topped Aster (x2/5)
(flowers 1/2 - 3/4 in. wide and arranged in
fairly flat clusters)

37D Many-flowered Aster (x2/5)
(leaves narrow)

37E Sharp-leaved [Mountain or
Whorled] Aster (x2/5)
(upper leaves are larger than lower
leaves and appear to be whorled;
flowers white or purple tinged)

Leaves not Heart-shaped

38A Cape [Sickle-leaved]
Golden Aster (x2/5)
(leaves very narrow, rather
stiff, often curved,
4-12 in. high)

38B Maryland [Broad-leaved]
Golden Aster (x2/5) (leaves
oblong or lance shaped; 1-2
1/2 feet high)

38C Purple-stemmed Aster (x2/5)
(stem hairy and sometimes purple,
clasping leaves; flowers 1-1 1/2 in.
wide; plant 2-8 feet high)

38D Calico [Starved] Aster
(x2/5) (flowers white or
purple tinged; have 9-15
petals and often have some
purple disks)

38E New England Aster (x2/5) (stem
hairy, leaves lance-shaped, clasping;
flower 1-2 in.; violet purple,
occasionally rose colored or white)

Waterfall Photographs

39CT   Campbells Falls

Campbells Falls State Park
North Norfolk, CT - Litchfield County and
Southfield, MA - Berkshire County
See information on Pages 2 through 4.

40CT   Dean's Ravine

Housatonic State Forest
Canaan, CT
Litchfield County
See information on Pages 5 through 6.

41CT   Kent Falls (upper falls)

Kent Falls State Park
Kent, CT
Litchfield County
See information on Pages 6 through 9.

42CT   Pine Swamp Brook Falls

Sharon, CT
Litchfield County
See information on Pages 9 through 10.

43CT   Prydden Brook Falls

Paugusett State Forest
Newtown, CT
Fairfield County
See information on Pages 10 through 12.

44MA   Bash Bish Falls

Bash Bish Falls State Park
Mount Washington, MA
Berkshire County
See information on Pages 16 through 18.

45MA   Bear's Den Falls

Bear's Den Reservation
New Salem, MA
Franklin County
See information on Pages 18 through 20.

46MA   Cascade Falls

North Adams, MA
Berkshire County
See information on Pages 20 through 22.

47MA   Chapelbrook Falls

Chapelbrook Reservation
South Ashfield, MA
Franklin County
See information on Pages 22 through 23.

48MA Gunn Brook Falls

Sunderland, MA
Franklin County
See information on Pages 24 through 25.

49MA   Peck's Brook Falls (upper and middle falls)

Adams, MA
Berkshire County
See information on Pages 37 through 39.

50MA   Peck's Brook Falls (lower falls)

Adams, MA
Berkshire County
See information on Pages 37 through 39.

51MA   Sanderson Brook Falls

Chester-Blandford State Forest
Chester and Blandford, MA
Hampden County
See information on Pages 40 through 41.

52MA Slatestone Brook Falls

Sunderland, MA
Franklin County
See information on Pages 41 through 42.

53MA   Wahconah Falls
Wahconah Falls State Park
Dalton, MA
Berkshire County
See information on Pages 43 through 44.

54NY Ashley Falls
North-South Lake Area of the Catskill Forest Preserve
Haines Falls, NY
Greene County
See information on Pages 48 through 49.

55NY   Kaaterskill Falls

Catskill Forest Preserve
Haines Falls and Palenville, NY
Greene County
See information on Pages 53 through 55.

56NY Plotter Kill Falls

Plotter Kill Nature and Historical Preserve
Rotterdam, NY
Schenectady County
See information on Pages 55 through 58.

57NY   Shelving Rock Falls
Lake George Trail System
Fort Ann, NY
Washington County
See information on Pages 60 through 62.

58VT   Moss Glen Falls

Granville, VT
Addison County
See information on Page 68.

59VT Texas Falls

Green Mountain National Forest
Hancock, VT
Addison County
Photo taken in mid April. Note ice on left bank.
See information on Pages 69 through 70.

The Norcross Wildlife Sanctuary at Tupper Hill

Monson and Wales, MA   Hampden County

See Driving Directions, What to Expect,
and Trail Information.

Early Season

Start by leaving the Visitors Center from the left side door. After the sidewalk, turn right onto a dirt road to a sign for the Short Trail; Yellow Wood Sorrel, Goldenrod, Daisy Fleabane [Sweet Scabious]

Follow sign for Short Trail through Hickory Grove: Goldenrod, Meadowsweet, Hairy Hawkweed

Go through gate to fenced-in area of Short Trail: Cup Plant [Indian Cup], Kousa [Japanese or Korean] Dogwood, Wild Quinine [American Feverfew], Oak Leaf Hydrangea, Great Blue Lobelia [Great Lobelia] (beginning to bloom), Great White Lobelia (beginning to bloom), Nodding Wild Onion, Fly Poison (green), Black Snakeroot [Black Cohosh] (near end of bloom), Wild Monkshood (near end of bloom), Purple-flowering Raspberry

Out other gate, across road, through Conifer Grove to Acid Rock Garden: Harebell [Bluebell]

Skip Upland Shrub Area and continue on trail: Cardinal Flower, White Wood Aster, Spotted Touch-me-not [Jewelweed] (one)

Lower Trail: Downy Rattlesnake Plantain

Right onto Boardwalk: Goldenrod

Pond Trail and trail to right around pond: Meadowsweet, Cardinal Flower, Goldenrod, Cattail, Steeplebush [Hardhack], Heather [Ling] (pink), Gray-headed Coneflower, Narrow-leaved Mountain Mint, Butterfly Weed [Pleurisy Root], Horsemint [Dotted Horsemint], Daisy Fleabane [Sweet Scabious], Common St. Johnswort, Meadow Beauty [Deergrass], Upland Aster [Upland White Aster], Blue Toadflax, Maryland Golden [Broad-leaved Golden] Aster, Poppy Mallow, Purple Gerardia, Rose Coreopsis [Pink Tickseed], Prickly Pear Cactus, Downy Skullcap, Swamp Milkweed, Showy Tick Trefoil (near end of bloom), Meadowsweet, Poppy Mallow (different type), Rough-fruited [Sulphur] Cinquefoil, Cape Golden [Sickle-leaved Golden] Aster, Fly Poison (green), Dillen's Tick Trefoil, Boneset [Thoroughwort], Spiked Lobelia, Selfheal [Heal-all]

Away from pond on boardwalk, turn right on boardwalk: Flat-topped Aster (white)

Turn right at Circle Garden: Hairy Wood Mint, Great Blue Lobelia [Great Lobelia], False Dragonhead [Obedient Plant], Black Snakeroot [Black Cohosh] (many), Bladder Campion, Golden Star

Up steps to turn left at edge of mowed field and continue right at edge: Wild Thyme, Rabbit-foot Clover, Stiff [Bristly] Aster, Spiked [Dense] Blazing Star

Field to left of bat house and right of Pine Barren Garden: Yellow Fringed Orchis [Yellow Fringed Orchid], Goldenrod, Common St. Johnswort, Selfheal [Heal-all], Heather [Ling], Spiked Lobelia, Stokes Blue Aster

Into Pine Barren Garden: Stokes Blue Aster, Goldenrod (many), Steeplebush [Hardhack], Heather [Ling], Spiked Lobelia, Shrubby Cinquefoil, Black-eyed Susan, Spiked [Dense] Blazing Star

Go back onto Lower Trail and take bridge left to Visitors Center: Goldenrod, Daisy Fleabane [Sweet Scabious], Wild Carrot [Queen Anne's Lace, Bird's Nest], Black-eyed Susan, Thin-leaved Coneflower

Middle of August

The Norcross Wildlife Sanctuary at Tupper Hill

Monson and Wales, MA   Hampden County

See Driving Directions, What to Expect,
and Trail Information.

Early Season

Start by leaving the Visitors Center from the left side door. After the sidewalk turn right and go up to the sign for the Short Trail: Pokeweed, Daisy Fleabane [Sweet Scabious] (near end of bloom), Goldenrod

Follow path to Short Trail through Hickory Grove: Hairy Hawkweed, White Wood Aster [Wood Aster], Goldenrod

Go through gate to fenced-in area of Short Trail: Cup Plant [Indian Cup] (near end of bloom), Goldenrod, Wild Quinine [American Feverfew], Mistflower, Oak Leaf Hydrangea, Great Blue Lobelia [Great Lobelia], Wild Petunia, Nodding Wild Onion (near end of bloom), Fly Poison (near end of bloom), White Wood Aster [Wood Aster], Wild Monkshood

Go through gate out of wildflower garden (Short Trail), cross road, go through Conifer Grove, past Acid Rock Garden, and Upland Shrub Area and continue towards Lower Trail: White Wood Aster [Wood Aster], Cardinal Flower (few), Goldenrod

Follow Lower Trail to Boardwalk. Turn right onto Boardwalk: White Wood Aster [Wood Aster], Spotted Touch-me-not [Jewelweed], Great Blue Lobelia [Great Lobelia]

Right onto Pond Trail: White Wood Aster [Wood Aster], Goldenrod, Cardinal Flower

Trail to right around pond: White Wood Aster [Wood Aster], Goldenrod, Cardinal Flower, Heather [Ling] (pink), Blue Curls, Gray-headed Coneflower, Horsemint [Dotted Horsemint], Narrow-leaved Mountain Mint, Upland White Aster [Upland Aster], Hairy Hawkweed, Rough Hawkweed, Field Hawkweed [King Devil], Common Evening Primrose, Prairie Golden Aster, Butterfly Weed [Pleurisy Root], Downy Skullcap, Rose Coreopsis [Pink Tickseed], Poppy Mallow, Mouse Ear, Common St. Johnswort (near end of bloom), Grass-leaved Blazing Star, Poppy Mallow (another type), Rough-fruited [Sulphur] Cinquefoil (near end of bloom), Cape Golden [Sickle-leaved Golden] Aster, Daisy Fleabane [Sweet Scabious], Sneezeweed, Boneset [Thoroughwort], Heart-leaved Skullcap, Showy Aster, Spiked Lobelia

Turn right to leave pond area. Turn right on boardwalk: White Wood Aster [Wood Aster], False Dragonhead [Obedient Plant]

Turn right after bridge and go to the Circle Garden: Great Blue Lobelia [Great Lobelia], Showy Coneflower, Hairy Wood Mint, Cardinal Flower, Goldenrod, Spotted Touch-me-not [Jewelweed]

Go up steps to field, turn left at edge of field and go right to continue following edge of field: Spotted Knapweed, Daisy Fleabane [Sweet Scabious], Rabbit-foot Clover (near end of bloom), Heather [Ling] , Stiff [Bristly] Aster (many), Spiked [Dense] Blazing Star, Birdsfoot Trefoil, Meadowsweet (near end of bloom), Common St. Johnswort (near end of bloom)

Field to left of bat house and right of Pine Barren Garden: Spiked Lobelia, Heather [Ling] (most purple, some white), Meadowsweet (near end of bloom), Steeplebush [Hardhack] (near end of bloom), Common St. Johnswort (near end of bloom), Yellow Fringed Orchis [Yellow Fringed Orchid], Canada St. Johnswort, Heath Aster (few)

Pine Barren Garden: Stiff [Bristly] Aster, Meadowsweet, Common St. Johnswort (many), Spiked Lobelia, Heather [Ling], Meadow Beauty [Deergrass] (one), Canada St. Johnswort, Shrubby Cinquefoil, Meadowsweet, Boneset [Thoroughwort] (one), Virginia Mountain Mint, Black-eyed Susan, Spiked [Dense] Blazing Star, Sweet Pepperbush, Showy Coneflower

Go back onto Lower Trail and take bridge left to Visitors Center.

Mount Greylock State Reservation

New Ashford and Cheshire, MA   Berkshire County

See Driving Directions, What to Expect,
and Trail Information.

Late Season

Jones Nose Trail - field: Yarrow [Milfoil] (near end of bloom), Buttercup, Goldenrod (many), Meadowsweet (quite a few), Purple-stemmed Aster, White Snakeroot, Fireweed [Great Willow Herb] (near end of bloom), Common St. Johnswort (near end of bloom), Orange Hawkweed [Devil's Paintbrush] (few), Silverrod, Steeplebush [Hardhack] (near end of bloom), Heart-leaved Aster, Canada Thistle (near end of bloom), Canada Hawkweed

Jones Nose Trail into woods: Pale Touch-me-not [Jewelweed], White Wood Aster, Wild Basil (few), Sharp-leaved [Whorled, Mountain] Aster, Zigzag [Broad-leaved] Goldenrod

Left on CCC Dynamite Trail: White Snakeroot

Turned around shortly after trail sign.

Beginning of September

High Ledges Wildlife Sanctuary

Shelburne, MA   Franklin County

See Driving Directions, What to Expect, and Trail Information.

Late Season

Flowers along road from parking lot back toward entrance a short distance (stop at woods).: Goldenrod, Yarrow [Milfoil], Red Clover, White Snakeroot, Tansy, Meadowsweet (near end of bloom), Calico [Starved] Aster (beginning to bloom), Boneset [Thoroughwort], Selfheal [Heal-all]

Waterthrush Trail to woods: Nothing new

Bear's Den Falls

Bear's Den Reservation
New Salem, MA   Franklin County

See Driving Directions, What to Expect,
and Trail Information.

Late Season

Wildflowers by trail to falls: White Wood Aster, Indian Pipe [Corpse Plant]

The Norcross Wildlife Sanctuary at Tupper Hill

Monson and Wales, MA   Hampden County

See Driving Directions, What to Expect,
and Trail Information.

Late Season

By parking lot: Spotted Touch-me-not [Jewelweed], Meadowsweet

Start by leaving the Visitors Center from the left side door. After the sidewalk turn right and then turn left at the sign to the Short Trail: Goldenrod, Meadowsweet, Spotted Touch-me-not [Jewelweed], White Wood [Wood] Aster

Trail to the Short Trail through the Hickory Grove: Some flowers seen before plus Smooth Aster (purple), Calico [Starved] Aster, Nipplewort

Through gate to fenced-in area of Short Trail: Smooth Aster (near end of bloom), Closed [Bottle] Gentian (beginning to bloom), Narrow-leaved Gentian (beginning to bloom), Mistflower, Great Blue Lobelia [Great Lobelia], Great White Lobelia, Pink Turtlehead, Wild Monkshood, Indian Pink

Gate out of wildflower garden (Short Trail), across the road and into the Conifer Grove: Yellow Stargrass

Acid Rock Garden: Spiked Lobelia, Harebell

Take Lower Trail, and then turn right onto the boardwalk. Turn right again at fork going to the Pond Trail. Go right around pond.: White Snakeroot, Heather [Ling] (pink - many), Gray-headed Coneflower, Horsemint [Dotted Horsemint], Narrow-leaved Mountain Mint, Downy Skullcap, Blue Curls, Sweet Everlasting [Catfoot], Common Evening Primrose, Prairie Golden Aster, Maryland Golden [Broad-leaved Golden] Aster, Poppy Mallow, Plymouth Gentian, Sneezeweed (many), Silverrod, Scarlet Monkey Flower, Cape Golden [Sickle-leaved Golden] Aster (quite a few), Spiked [Dense] Blazing Star, Cardinal Flower (quite a few), Heart-Leaved Skullcap, Rose Coreopsis [Pink Tickseed], Aromatic Aster

Down boardwalk away from pond and then take boardwalk to the right: Purple-stemmed Aster, Purple Milkwort

Path to right around the outside of the Circle Garden: Great Blue Lobelia [Great Lobelia], Great White Lobelia, Cardinal Flower, Purple-stemmed Aster, White Wood Aster [Wood Aster], False Dragonhead [Obedient Plant], White Snakeroot

Cross bridge with railing and go left on Lime Flower Cobbles,:   Showy Aster, White Wood Aster [Wood Aster], White Snakeroot, Wild Bleeding Heart, Violet, Calico [Starved] Aster

Back to bridge - turn left to go up steps to field: Yellow Wood Sorrel

Turn left near edge of field and then turn right to continue to follow the edge of the field.:   Flowers not seen before are Wild Thyme, Stiff [Bristly] Aster, New York Aster, Rabbit-foot Clover

Path into Pine Barren (from back):   Wild Quinine [American Feverfew], Shrubby St. Johnswort, Kalm's [Brook] Lobelia, Bog Aster, Pitcher Plant, Meadowsweet, Spiked [Dense] Blazing Star, Arrow-leaved Tearthumb, Steeplebush [Hardhack] (one), Bushy Aster (lavender, blue, and white - beginning to bloom), Boneset [Thoroughwort] (near end of bloom), Black-eyed Susan, Red Clover

Go back to Lower Trail and take bridge left to Visitors Center.

Middle of September

High Ledges Wildlife Sanctuary

Shelburne, MA   Franklin County

See Driving Directions, What to Expect, and Trail Information.

Late Season

Near parking lot: Goldenrod, Calico [Starved] Aster, Meadowsweet, New England Aster

Road past iron bar barrier: Goldenrod, Calico [Starved] Aster, New England Aster, Meadowsweet, Red Clover, Lowrie's Aster, White Wood Aster, Daisy Fleabane [Sweet Scabious], White Snakeroot, Blue-stemmed [Wreath] Goldenrod, Zigzag [Broad-leaved] Goldenrod, Silverrod

Skip Lady's Slipper Trail on right, skip West Brook Trail on left.: Sharp-leaved [Mountain, Whorled] Aster (near end of bloom)

Take left fork, then take right fork past cabin and continue to the right. Here you will see an excellent view from the ledges area. Pass the Lady's Slipper Trail sign and follow the blue circles on trees. Continue following the Lady's Slipper Trail sign to the right. Bear right again at the Lady's Slipper Trail sign. Do not go on the North Trail. Cross a small brook. Don't take the Wolves Den Trail on the left. Cross another tiny stream. Turn left at the second Wolves Den Trail.: Horse Balm [Richweed, Stoneroot], Boott's Rattlesnake Root

After that you will see another Wolves Den Trail sign pointing to the left. Do not go left there, but go straight into the Gentian Swamp.:   Spotted Touch-me-not [Jewelweed], Turtlehead, Purple-stemmed Aster, Grass-of-Parnassus, Pitcher Plant, Peppermint, Selfheal [Heal-all], Shrubby Cinquefoil

Go back to the Lady's Slipper Trail and turn left. Trail signs change to yellow indicating that you are going back toward the parking lot. Cross wooden bridge with no railing. Turn left following the yellow circles.   Then turn left and go up the road to the parking area.

Meadow area beside the road between the parking lot and the Waterthrush Trail entrance: The same flowers as those by the parking area plus Red Clover, White Snakeroot, Small White Aster, Yarrow [Milfoil], Selfheal [Heal-all], Boneset [Thoroughwort] (near end of bloom)

End of September

Norcross Wildlife Sanctuary at Tupper Hill

Monson and Wales, MA   Hampden County

See Driving Directions, What to Expect,
and Trail Information.

Late Season

By parking lot: Goldenrod, Meadowsweet, Wild Thyme

Start by leaving the Visitors Center from the left side door. After the sidewalk turn right, and then turn left at the sign to the Short Trail.: Goldenrod, Small White Aster, White Wood Aster, Calico [Starved] Aster

Follow path through Hickory Grove to Short Trail: Some flowers mentioned before plus Smooth Aster (purple, light purple), Blue-stemmed [Wreath] Goldenrod

Go through gate to fenced-in area of Short Trail: Smooth Aster, Closed [Bottle] Gentian (many), Pink Turtlehead, Great Blue Lobelia [Great Lobelia] (near end of bloom), Great White Lobelia (near end of bloom), Blue-stemmed [Wreath]

Goldenrod, Sampson's Snakeroot [Striped Gentian], Wild Monkshood (near end of bloom), White Wood Aster [Wood Aster]

Go out other gate and continue across road into Conifer Grove: New flower - Lowrie's Aster (light purple)

Go past Acid Rock Garden and past Upland Shrub area. Turn right at the sign pointing to where you have already been and saying "Upland Shrubs   Short Trail": Purple-stemmed Aster

Bear left at the next signs toward "Boardwalk, Lime Cobbles, and Pine Barren Garden." Turn right on boardwalk, then right again onto Pond Trail.: Boott's Rattlesnake Root

Trail to right around pond: White Snakeroot, Heather [Ling] (pink), Bushy Aster, Sweet Everlasting [Catfoot], Rough Hawkweed, Daisy Fleabane [Sweet Scabious], Horsemint [Dotted Horsemint], Narrow-leaved Mountain Mint, Field Hawkweed [King Devil] (one), Prairie Golden Aster, Smooth Aster, Plymouth Gentian, Cardinal Flower (near end of bloom), Downy Skullcap, Silverrod, Rose Coreopsis [Pink Tickseed] (near end of bloom), Late Purple [Spreading] Aster, Ironweed, Cape Golden [Sickle-leaved Golden] Aster (near end of bloom), Sneezeweed, Yellow Wood Sorrel, Gray-headed Coneflower

Back onto boardwalk - then turn right. Turn right again at end of boardwalk and go around Circle Garden. White Snakeroot, Purple-stemmed Aster, Cardinal Flower (near end of bloom), White Wood Aster [Wood Aster], Goldenrod, Great Blue Lobelia [Great Lobelia] (near end of bloom), Spiked Lobelia (near end of bloom)

Left into Circle Garden and then continue toward bridge: Indian Tobacco (near end of bloom)

Cross bridge (towards steps) and turn left into Lime Flower Cobble area: White Snakeroot, Showy Aster (bright violet), Closed [Bottle] Gentian, Wild Bleeding Heart (near end of bloom)

Go back to wooden steps and go up to the field. Then turn left to walk near edge of field.: Wild Thyme, Spotted Knapweed, Bushy Aster, Sweet Everlasting [Catfoot], Goldenrod, Rabbit-foot Clover, Red Clover

Turn right to continue following edge of field.: Spiked [Dense] Blazing Star, Grass-leaved Blazing Star

Turn left to take path into Pine Barren.: Shrubby St. Johnswort, Pine Barren Gentian, Heather [Ling], Autumn Ladies' Tresses, Nuttall's Lobelia, Bog Aster, New York Aster, Round-leaved Boneset, Shrubby Cinquefoil, Fringed Gentian, Black-eyed Susan (near end of bloom), Heart-leaved Aster, Grass-leaved Blazing Star

Back onto Lower Trail: Nipplewort

Turn left at sign "Boardwalk, Lime Cobbles, Pine Barren Garden" to go back to Visitors Center: Thin-leaved Coneflower (many), Black-eyed Susan (few)

Pecks Brook Falls

Adams, MA   Berkshire County

See Driving Directions, What to Expect,
and Trail Information.

Late Season

Trail to falls: White Wood Aster (near end of bloom), White Snakeroot, Heart-leaved Aster, Panicled Aster, Goldenrod, Purple-stemmed Aster, Wild Carrot [Queen Anne's Lace, Bird's Nest] (near end of bloom), Daisy Fleabane [Sweet Scabious], Calico [Starved] Aster

Flowers beside Pecks Brook near the lower falls: Pale Touch-me-not [Jewelweed], Herb Robert

Beginning of October

Mount Greylock State Reservation

New Ashford and Cheshire, MA   Berkshire County

See Driving Directions, What to Expect,
and Trail Information.

Early Season

Jones Nose Trail through short wooded area and large field: Panicled Aster, Calico [Starved] Aster, Heart-leaved Aster (many in spots), White Snakeroot, Purple-stemmed Aster (quite a few), Common St. Johnswort (near end of bloom), Goldenrod (near end of bloom), Yarrow [Milfoil] (near end of bloom), Lowrie's Aster, Maiden Pink (near end of bloom), Canada Hawkweed (near end of bloom)

Into woods: Some flowers seen before plus White Wood Aster, Sharp-leaved [Whorled, Mountain] Aster (one)

Turned around before CCC Dynamite Trail.

Middle of October

Mount Sugarloaf State Reservation

South Deerfield, MA   Franklin County

See Driving Directions, What to Expect,
and Trail Information.

Early Season

Trail from lower parking lot: Heart-leaved Aster (many),
Lady's Thumb (many), White Campion, Goldenrod (near end
of bloom), Blue-stemmed [Wreath] Goldenrod, White Wood
Aster, Swamp Smartweed, Calico [Starved] Aster, Lowrie's
Aster (few), Daisy Fleabane [Sweet Scabious]

Into woods: No new flowers

Down road to right: Heart-leaved Aster, White Wood Aster,
Blue-stemmed [Wreath] Goldenrod, White Snakeroot (near
end of bloom), Zigzag [Broad-leaved] Goldenrod, Harebell
[Bluebell] (one)

High Ledges Wildlife Sanctuary

Shelburne, MA   Franklin County

See Driving Directions, What to Expect,
and Trail Information.

Early Season

Area by parking lot and down dirt road past iron bar: New
England Aster, White Wood Aster (many), Calico [Starved]
Aster (quite a few), Smooth Aster (one), Lowrie's Aster, Red
Clover, Heart-leaved Aster (quite a few), Blue-stemmed

[Wreath] Goldenrod (near end of bloom), Wild Carrot [Queen Anne's Lace, Bird's Nest] (few), Zigzag [Broad-leaved] Goldenrod (near end of bloom - few), White Snakeroot (few), Silverrod (near end of bloom), Goldenrod (few - near end of bloom)

Lady's Slipper Trail: White Lettuce (few)

Across wooden bridge and to the left: No new flowers

Back to road and left to parking area: No new flowers

Norcross Wildlife Sanctuary at Tupper Hill

Monson and Wales, MA   Hampden County

See Driving Directions, What to Expect,
and Trail Information.

Late Season

Begin by leaving the Visitors Center from the left side door. After the sidewalk turn right and then go left into the Hickory Grove following the sign to the Short Trail: Calico [Starved] Aster (near end of bloom), Goldenrod (near end of bloom), Wavy-leaved Aster, White Wood Aster [Wood Aster] (near end of bloom), Heart-leaved Aster

Through gate to fenced-in area of Short Trail: Smooth Aster (purplish-blue), Showy Aster, White Snakeroot, Pink Turtlehead (near end of bloom), Closed [Bottle] Gentian (near end of bloom)

Go out other gate: Lowrie's Aster

Continue across road, through Conifer Grove, onto Lower Trail, and follow Boardwalk to the Pond Trail. Take Pond Trail to the right and go to the right around the pond.: White Wood Aster [Wood Aster] (near end of bloom), Calico [Starved] Aster (one), Bushy Aster (quite a few in one spot), Pearly Everlasting [Catfoot] (near end of bloom), Small White Aster, Heather [Ling] (violet) (near end of bloom), Prairie Golden Aster (some near end of bloom), Aromatic Aster, Goldenrod, Scaly Blazing Star, Rough-fruited Cinquefoil (one), Sneezeweed

Go back out of pond area to Boardwalk. Take first right turn on Boardwalk. Turn right after bridge and go around Circle Garden.: White Wood Aster [Wood Aster] (near end of bloom)

Over bridge and to the left into and around Lime Fern Cobbles.: Showy Aster, White Wood Aster [Wood Aster]

Up steps to field and go to left near edge of field. Turn right to continue around field.: Bushy Aster, Showy Aster, Pine Barren Gentian

Follow trail sign going the opposite way of the arrow into the woods. This is called Cedar Swamp on the map. Follow trail to fence beside Meadow Garden. Continue beside fence.: Purple-stemmed Aster, New England Aster (near end of bloom), Fringed Gentian, Many-flowered Aster

Turn around and come back to first field. Follow trail signs into the Pine Barren area.: Bushy Aster (many), Pine Barren Gentian, New York Aster (near end of bloom), Autumn Ladies' Tresses, Fringed Gentian

Back to Visitors Center (continue from Pine Barren onto Lower Trail and then turn left at sign on right "Boardwalk, Lime Cobbles and Pine Barren Garden").:   Showy Coneflower, Goldenrod

New York

Middle of April

Kaaterskill Falls

Catskill Forest Preserve
Haines Falls and Palenville, NY   Greene County

See Driving Directions, What to Expect,
and Trail Information.

Late Season

Trail to Kaaterskill Falls: Coltsfoot

Beginning of May

Bog Meadow Brook Nature Trail

Saratoga Springs, NY   Saratoga County

See Driving Directions, What to Expect,
and Trail Information.

Late Season

Beginning of Trail: Skunk Cabbage (near end of bloom - many plants), Marsh Marigold [Cowslip] (scattered patches)

Over bridge with handrail: Common Shadbush, Wild Strawberry, Smooth Shadbush, Violet (white), Wood Anemone [Windflower] (beginning to bloom)

Small 1 mile (1MI) marker on tree to right: Mayapple
[Mandrake]

Turned around at sign on left saying "Bog Meadow Brook
Forested Wetland Habitat."

Railroad Run

Saratoga Springs, NY   Saratoga County

See Driving Directions, What to Expect,
and Trail Information.

Late Season

Blacktop trail on right side: Golden Charm Tulip, flowering
fruit trees (pink and white), Daffodil [Narcissus] (white,
yellow, and combination of white and yellow), Tulip (pinkish-
red), Dutch [Common] Hyacinth (white, light pink)

Turn around at next road to go back on the other side: No new
flowers except Tulip (purple).

Kaaterskill Falls

Catskill Forest Preserve
Haines Falls and Palenville, NY   Greene County

See Driving Directions, What to Expect,
and Trail Information.

Late Season

Wildflowers near the left side of Route 23A (walking from
parking lot to Kaaterskill Falls Trail): Smooth Shadbush,

Smooth Pussytoes, Plantain-leaved Pussytoes, Strawberry

Trail to Kaaterskill Falls: Hobblebush (scattered patches), Wake-robin [Birthroot, Purple or Red Trillium]

End of May

Railroad Run

Saratoga Springs, NY   Saratoga County

See Driving Directions, What to Expect, and Trail Information.

Late Season

Blacktop trail on right side: Tulip (several colors - few), flowering tree (pink), Blue Flax (quite a few), Strawberry, Violet (purple), Ground Ivy [Gill-over-the-ground], Apple tree and another fruit tree (near end of bloom), Hairy Rock Cress, Morrow's Honeysuckle, Common Winter Cress [Yellow Rocket]

Turn around at next road to go back on the other side: Some flowers seen before plus Bird [Pin, Fire] Cherry (near end of bloom)

Bog Meadow Brook Nature Trail

Saratoga Springs, NY   Saratoga County

See Driving Directions, What to Expect, and Trail Information.

Late Season

Nature Trail: Strawberry (many), Wild Geranium [Spotted Cranesbill] (beginning to bloom), Morrow's Honeysuckle (many), Wood Anemone [Windflower], Highbush [Swamp] Blueberry, Nodding Trillium, Chokecherry, Hybrid of Morrow's and Tartarian Honeysuckle, Red Chokeberry

Over bridge with handrail: Tartarian Honeysuckle, Wild Ginger, Violet (light purplish-blue, medium purple), Wake-robin [Birthroot, Purple or Red Trillium], Canada Mayflower [Wild Lily-of-the-valley] (beginning to bloom), Starflower (beginning to bloom), Bellwort, Star-flowered Solomon's Seal (beginning to bloom), Early Low Blueberry, Wild Sarsaparilla (beginning to bloom), Yellow Clintonia [Bluebead] (beginning to bloom), Marsh Marigold [Cowslip] (few), White Baneberry [Doll's Eyes]

Turn around at one mile (1 MI) marker on tree to the right.

Kaaterskill Falls

Catskill Forest Preserve
Haines Falls and Palenville, NY   Greene County

See Driving Directions, What to Expect,
and Trail Information.

Late Season

Wildflowers near the left side of Route 23A (walking from parking lot to Kaaterskill Falls Trail.): Smooth Pussytoes, Plantain-leaved Pussytoes

Trail to Kaaterskill Falls: Dwarf Raspberry, Yellow Clintonia [Bluebead] (many in one spot), Baneberry (beginning to bloom), Jack-in-the-pulpit [Indian Turnip], Striped Maple tree, Foamflower [False Miterwort] (many in spots), Violet (light purple), Starflower (few - beginning to bloom), Red-berried Elder (two)

Beginning of June

Bog Meadow Brook Nature Trail

Saratoga Springs, NY   Hampden County

See Driving Directions, What to Expect,
and Trail Information.

Late Season

By parking area: Wild Geranium [Spotted Cranesbill], Common Winter Cress [Yellow Rocket]

Nature Trail: Wild Geranium [Spotted Cranesbill] (many), Blunt-leaved [Grove] Sandwort (many), Morrow's Honeysuckle (many), Common Cinquefoil (many), Dwarf Raspberry (near end of bloom), Strawberry, Wild Sarsaparilla (look under leaves - beginning to bloom), Hairy Rock Cress, Chokecherry, Golden Ragwort, Hybrid of Morrow's and Tartarian Honeysuckle, Swamp Dewberry, Buttercup, Red-osier Dogwood, Tartarian Honeysuckle, Russian-olive shrub, Blue-eyed Grass, Common Blackberry, Spatterdock [Yellow Pond Lily, Cow Lily], Violet (light purple), Yarrow [Milfoil] (beginning to bloom), Common Winter Cress [Yellow Rocket], False Solomon's Seal [Wild Spikenard], Canada Mayflower [Wild Lily-of-the-valley] (quite a few in two spots), Yellow Clintonia [Bluebead] (quite a few in many spots), Starflower, Early Low Blueberry (few), Bellwort (one), Highbush [Swamp] Blueberry (one), Mayapple [Mandrake] (many), Violet (medium blue)

Turn around just a little after the one mile "1 MI" marker on a tree to the right.

Railroad Run

Saratoga Springs, NY   Saratoga County

See Driving Directions, What to Expect,
and Trail Information.

Late Season

Blacktop trail on right side: Blue Flax, Strawberry, Bittersweet Nightshade, Ground Ivy [Gill-over-the-ground], Rugosa Rose, Silvery Cinquefoil, White Campion, Bladder Campion, Yarrow [Milfoil], Hairy Rock Cress, Yellow Sweet Clover (beginning to bloom), Pink (with flowers in a spike), Red Clover, Oxeye Daisy, Blue-eyed Grass (few), Cow [Tufted] Vetch (beginning to bloom)

Turn around at next road to go back on the other side: Morrow's Honeysuckle, Blue Flax, Cow [Tufted] Vetch, Oxeye Daisy, Yarrow [Milfoil] (white, a few pink), Bladder Campion, Strawberry, Hairy Rock Cress, Spiderwort, Blue-eyed Grass, Pink (with flowers in a spike), Yellow Sweet Clover, Silvery Cinquefoil, Red Clover, Field Pansy

Harlem Valley Rail Trail

Millerton, NY   Dutchess County

See Driving Directions, What to Expect,
and Trail Information.

Late Season

Blacktop trail: Dame's Violet [Dame's Rocket] (many),
Cypress Spurge, Buttercup, Ground Ivy [Gill-over-the-
ground] (many), Field Hawkweed [King Devil] (beginning to
bloom), Morrow's Honeysuckle, Celandine (many), Red-osier
Dogwood, Wild Geranium [Spotted Cranesbill], Mouse Ear

First bridge: Burning Bush [Wahoo], Alternate-leaved
Dogwood (several - beginning to bloom), Garden Valerian
[Garden Heliotrope] (pink)

Cross road and second bridge: No new flowers.

Trail surrounded by rocks on both sides: Jack-in-the-pulpit
[Indian Turnip], False Solomon's Seal [Wild Spikenard]
(beginning to bloom), Small-flowered Crowfoot, Hybrid of
Morrow's and Tartarian Honeysuckle

Third bridge: White Campion (beginning to bloom), Tower
Mustard, Common Winter Cress [Yellow Rocket], Strawberry,
Honewort, Weigela (red), Trumpet [Coral] Honeysuckle

Past private driveway: Golden Alexanders

Turn around shortly after driveway.

End of June

Railroad Run

Saratoga Springs, NY   Saratoga County
See Driving Directions, What to Expect,
and Trail Information.

Late Season

<u>Blacktop trail on right side</u>:   Blue Flax (many), Yarrow [Milfoil] (many - mostly white, a few pink), Daisy Fleabane [Sweet Scabious], Rugosa Rose (quite a few), Yellow Goatsbeard, Red Clover, Yellow Sweet Clover (many), Bladder Campion (many), Blanket Flower (many), Rough-fruited [Sulphur] Cinquefoil, Bittersweet Nightshade, White Campion, Lance-leaved Coreopsis (double), Birdsfoot Trefoil, Alfalfa [Lucerne], Oxeye Daisy, Viper's Bugloss [Blueweed], Cow [Tufted] Vetch, Yellow Wood Sorrel

<u>Turn around at next road and come back on the other side.</u>
<u>Right side of trail was mowed</u>: No new flowers.

Bog Meadow Brook Nature Trail

Saratoga Springs, NY   Saratoga County

See Driving Directions, What to Expect,
and Trail Information.

Late Season

<u>By parking area</u>:   Yarrow [Milfoil], Yellow Iris, Wild Geranium [Spotted Cranesbill] (near end of bloom), Lady's Thumb, Wild Parsnip, Buttercup

<u>Nature Trail</u>: Common Cinquefoil, Yellow Wood Sorrel, Wild Geranium [Spotted Cranesbill] (near end of bloom), Buttercup, Blunt-leaved [Grove] Sandwort, Yarrow [Milfoil] (beginning to bloom), Red Clover, Swamp Dewberry, Common Elder, Field Hawkweed [King Devil], Tall Meadow Rue (buds), Daisy Fleabane [Sweet Scabious], Yellow Wood Sorrel, Oxeye Daisy, Red-osier Dogwood, Birdsfoot Trefoil, Silvery Cinquefoil

<u>Over bridge with handrail</u>: Hairy Rock Cress, Bittersweet Nightshade, Spatterdock [Yellow Pond Lily, Cow Lily], Bush Honeysuckle, Indian Hemp, Panicled [Gray] Dogwood, Larger Blue Flag Iris (few), Whorled [Four-leaved] Loosestrife

<u>Turn around at 1.0 mile (1 MI) marker on tree to right</u>: Maple-leaved Viburnum [Dockmackie]

Harlem Valley Rail Trail

Millerton, NY   Dutchess County

See Driving Directions, What to Expect,
and Trail Information.

Late Season

<u>Blacktop trail</u>: Dame's Violet [Dame's Rocket], Multiflora Rose (many in places - most white, some pink), Yellow Sweet Clover, Yellow Wood Sorrel, Rough-fruited [Sulphur] Cinquefoil (many in one area), Field Hawkweed [King Devil], Daisy Fleabane [Sweet Scabious], Red Clover, Bladder Campion, Tower Mustard, Oxeye Daisy, Ground Ivy [Gill-over-the-ground], Common Blackberry (many in places - near end of bloom), Nipplewort (many in places)

Over first bridge: Celandine (many in places), Swamp Valerian, Clematis (rosy-purple)

Cross road and second bridge: Bittersweet Nightshade

Third bridge: Wild Parsnip (beginning to bloom - few), Chicory (few), Birdsfoot Trefoil, Buttercup, Garden Rose (white, red), Trumpet [Coral] Honeysuckle, Weigela (red, white)

Past private driveway: Herb Robert (many)

Turn around at building with greenhouse attached to it.

Beginning of July

Ashley Falls

North-South Lake   Catskill Forest Preserve
Haines Falls, NY   Greene County

See Driving Directions, What to Expect,
and Trail Information.

Late Season

Flowers along the road to Mary's Glen Trail: Yellow Sweet Clover, Mountain Laurel, Birdsfoot Trefoil, Wild Thyme, Maiden Pink, Selfheal [Heal-all], Buttercup, Oxeye Daisy

Wildflower leaves along Mary's Glen Trail: Hobblebush (leaves), Touch-me-not [Jewelweed] (leaves), Foamflower [False Miterwort] (leaves), Jack-in-the-pulpit [Indian Turnip] (leaves), Yellow Clintonia [Bluebead] (leaves), Common Wood Sorrel (leaves)

Middle of July

Bog Meadow Brook Nature Trail

Saratoga Springs, NY   Saratoga County

See Driving Directions, What to Expect,
and Trail Information.

Late Season

By parking area: Swamp Smartweed (many), Purple
Loosestrife (many), Day Lily (many), Field Sow Thistle,
Hedge Bindweed, Yarrow [Milfoil] (near end of bloom), Wild
Carrot [Queen Anne's Lace, Bird's Nest], Wild Parsnip,
Fringed Loosestrife, Birdsfoot Trefoil, Oxeye Daisy (few),
Canada Lily [Meadow Lily, Wild Yellow Lily] (two),
Common Evening Primrose

Nature Trail (mowed beside path):   Canada Lily [Meadow
Lily, Wild Yellow Lily], Tall Meadow Rue, Yellow Wood
Sorrel, Fringed Loosestrife, Selfheal [Heal-all], Yarrow
[Milfoil], Red Clover, Meadowsweet, Common St. Johnswort,
Agrimony (one), White Sweet Clover, Swamp Rose,
Thimbleweed [Tall Anemone], Deptford Pink, Common
Mullein, Purple Loosestrife, Rough Cinquefoil, Daisy
Fleabane [Sweet Scabious], Oxeye Daisy, Paniceled Tick
Trefoil (one), Birdsfoot Trefoil, Wild Carrot [Queen Anne's
Lace, Bird's Nest] (beginning to bloom), Wild Lettuce, Wild
Parsnip, Bouncing Bet [Soapwort] (one)

Over bridge with handrail: Common Elder (near end of
bloom), Bittersweet Nightshade, Common Milkweed (few),
Smooth Rose, Swamp Dewberry (one), Swamp Milkweed
(one)

Turn around at 1.0 mile (1 MI) marker on tree to right.

Railroad Run

Saratoga Springs, NY   Saratoga County

See Driving Directions, What to Expect,
and Trail Information.

Late Season

Blacktop trail on right side: Blanket Flower (many - some near end of bloom), Spotted Knapweed (many), Yarrow [Milfoil] (some near end of bloom), White Sweet Clover (many), Lance-leaved Coreopsis (near end of bloom), Day Lily (various colors), Rugosa Rose, Daisy Fleabane [Sweet Scabious] (many), Gloriosa Daisy, Chicory, Wild Carrot [Queen Anne's Lace, Bird's Nest], Common St. Johnswort, Yellow Sweet Clover, Red Clover, Black-eyed Susan, Bouncing Bet [Soapwort] (light pink and white), Goldenrod (beginning to bloom), Lily, Rough-fruited [Sulphur] Cinquefoil, Cow [Tufted] Vetch, Bladder Campion (most finished), Slender Bush Clover, Bachelor's Button, Rose Coreopsis [Pink Tickseed], Rabbit-foot Clover, Viper's Bugloss [Blueweed], Common Mullein, Birdsfoot Trefoil, Common Milkweed

Turn around at next road and come back on the other side: Some flowers mentioned before plus Purple Coneflower

Harlem Valley Rail Trail

Millerton, NY   Dutchess County

See Driving Directions, What to Expect,
and Trail Information.

Late Season

Blacktop trail: Chicory, Birdsfoot Trefoil, Red Clover, Rough-fruited [Sulphur] Cinquefoil, Yellow Wood Sorrel, Wild Carrot [Queen Anne's Lace, Bird's Nest], Deptford Pink, Common Milkweed, Buttercup, Daisy Fleabane [Sweet Scabious], Wild Basil, Tall Meadow Rue

First bridge: Celandine (quite a few), Nipplewort (many), White Avens, Selfheal [Heal-all], Common St. Johnswort, Pale Touch-me-not [Jewelweed] (one - beginning to bloom)

Cross Road and second bridge: Dame's Violet [Dame's Rocket] (near end of bloom), Spotted Touch-me-not [Jewelweed] (beginning to bloom)

Third bridge: Bladder Campion (near end of bloom), Common Mullein, Wild Parsnip, Day Lily (orange - scattered - many in two places), Oxeye Daisy, Yellow Sweet Clover, Thimbleweed [Tall Anemone] (greenish petals), Rose (magenta - near end of bloom), Rose (very pale pink - near end of bloom), Trumpet [Coral] Honeysuckle, White Campion

Past private driveway: White Sweet Clover, Herb Robert

Turn around at building with greenhouse attached to it.

End of July

Shelving Rock Falls

Lake George Trail System
Fort Ann, NY   Washington County

See Driving Directions, What to Expect,
and Trail Information.

Late Season

Wildflowers and wildflower plants by the trail to the falls:
Selfheal [Heal-all], Yellow Clintonia [Bluebead] (leaves
only), Smooth False Foxglove, Indian Pipe [Corpse Plant],
Buttercup, Purple Loosestrife, Herb Robert

Ashley Falls

North-South Lake   Catskill Forest Preserve
Haines Falls, NY   Greene County

See Driving Directions, What to Expect,
and Trail Information.

Late Season

Flowers along the road to Mary's Glen Trail: Oxeye Daisy,
Wild Thyme, Selfheal [Heal-all], Birdsfoot Trefoil, Spotted
Joe-Pye Weed, Meadowsweet, Red Clover, Yellow Sweet
Clover, Rough-fruited [Sulphur] Cinquefoil, Maiden Pink
(quite a few), Tower Mustard

Flowers, buds, and leaves along Mary's Glen Trail:
Buttercup, Helleborine (buds), Spotted Joe-Pye Weed (buds),
Hobblebush (leaves), Spotted Touch-me-not [Jewelweed]

(beginning to bloom), Common Wood Sorrel (leaves), Violet (leaves), Sharp-leaved [Mountain, Whorled] Aster (buds), Foamflower [False Miterwort] (leaves), Wood Nettle, White Wood Aster (buds), Early Meadow Rue (leaves and berries), Virginia Waterleaf (finished), Jack-in-the-pulpit [Indian Turnip] (leaves)

Kaaterskill Falls

Catskill Forest Preserve
Haines Falls, NY   Greene County

See Driving Directions, What to Expect,
and Trail Information.

Late Season

Wildflowers near the left side of Route 23A (walking from parking lot to Kaaterskill Falls Trail.): Goldenrod, Spotted Knapweed, Daisy Fleabane [Sweet Scabious], Yellow Sweet Clover (many in one place), Smooth False Foxglove (quite a few), Deptford Pink, Common St. Johnswort, Wild Carrot [Queen Anne's Lace, Bird's Nest], Yarrow [Milfoil], Oxeye Daisy, Birdsfoot Trefoil, Crown Vetch [Axseed], (many in spots), White Sweet Clover, Purple-flowering Raspberry, Meadowsweet

Trail to Kaaterskill Falls: Spotted Touch-me-not [Jewelweed] (beginning to bloom), Selfheal [Heal-all], Wild Basil, Canada Hawkweed, Purple-flowering Raspberry, Common Wood Sorrel (leaves), Sharp-leaved [Mountain, Whorled] Aster (buds), Wood Nettle, Pale Touch-me-not [Jewelweed] (beginning to bloom)

Beginning of August

Plotter Kill Falls

Plotter Kill Nature and Historic Preserve
Rotterdam, NY   Schenectady County

See Driving Directions, What to Expect,
and Trail Information.

Late Season

Red Trail (beginning on the boardwalk):   Common St. Johnswort, Wild Carrot [Queen Anne's Lace, Bird's Nest], Selfheal [Heal-all], Motherwort, White Avens, Yellow Wood Sorrel, Buttercup, Spiked Lobelia, Purple-leaved Willow Herb, Enchanter's Nightshade, Northern Bugleweed, Rough Cinquefoil, Bittersweet Nightshade, Maple-leaved Viburnum (berries), Fringed Loosestrife, White Wood Aster, False Solomon's Seal [Wild Spikenard] (berries), Daisy Fleabane [Sweet Scabious], Spotted Knapweed, Goldenrod

Down Yellow Trail to cascade and second falls: Indian Pipe [Corpse Plant], Early Meadow Rue (berries), Purple or Red Trillium (gone to seed), Schreber's Aster, Hog Peanut

Back up to Red Trail and turn right to continue to third falls: No new flowers.

Harlem Valley Rail Trail

Millerton, NY   Dutchess County

See Driving Directions, What to Expect,
and Trail Information.

Late Season

Blacktop trail (beginning of trail was mowed): Chicory (many in places), Wild Carrot [Queen Anne's Lace, Bird's Nest] (many in places), Yellow Wood Sorrel (many), Spotted Touch-me-not [Jewelweed] (many), Goldenrod, Wild Balsam Apple [Wild Cucumber], Red Clover, Deptford Pink, Selfheal [Heal-all], Purple Loosestrife, Wild Basil, Daisy Fleabane [Sweet Scabious], Bladder Campion, Prickly Lettuce, Smooth Hawksbeard, Spotted Knapweed (quite a few in spots), Wild Bergamot (few), Rough-fruited [Sulphur] Cinquefoil (few)

First bridge: Celandine, Spiked Lobelia, Boneset [Thoroughwort] (one), White Avens, Pale Touch-me-not [Jewelweed], Common St. Johnswort, Common Evening Primrose, Clematis (rosy-purple), Hemlock Parsley

Cross road and second bridge: Nipplewort (many), Dame's Violet [Dame's Rocket] (few - near end of bloom), Bittersweet Nightshade, Wild Parsnip (near end of bloom)

Third bridge: Tall [Green-headed] Coneflower (two), Bouncing Bet [Soapwort] (white and light pink), Dittany, White Sweet Clover, Common Mullein (one), Birdsfoot Trefoil, Meadowsweet (one), Oxeye Daisy (near end of bloom), Lady's Thumb, Yellow Sweet Clover, Butter-and-eggs (beginning to bloom), Climbing Rose (white), Trumpet [Coral] Honeysuckle

Past private driveway: Cynthia (beginning to bloom), White Snakeroot (quite a few - beginning to bloom), Spotted St. Johnswort (few), Tall Blue Lettuce, Herb Robert (near end of bloom), White Vervain (one)

Turn around at building with greenhouse attached.

Ashley Falls

North-South Lake   Catskill Forest Preserve
Haines Falls, NY   Greene County

See Driving Directions, What to Expect,
and Trail Information.

Late Season

Flowers along the road to Mary's Glen Trail: Goldenrod, Wild Thyme, Red Clover, White Wood Aster, Sharp-leaved [Mountain, Whorled] Aster, Spotted Joe-Pye Weed, Spotted Touch-me-not [Jewelweed], Yellow Sweet Clover, Silvery Cinquefoil, Common St. Johnswort, Spotted Knapweed, Maiden Pink, Oxeye Daisy, Rough-fruited [Sulphur] Cinquefoil, Daisy Fleabane [Sweet Scabious]

Flowers and buds seen from Mary's Glen Trail: White Wood Aster, Calico [Starved] Aster, Purple-stemmed Aster (beginning to bloom), Spotted Joe-Pye Weed, Spotted Touch-me-not [Jewelweed] (beginning to bloom), Wood Nettle

Kaaterskill Falls

Catskill Forest Preserve
Haines Falls, NY   Greene County

See Driving Directions, What to Expect,
and Trail Information.

Late Season

Near the left side of Route 23A (walking from parking lot to Kaaterskill Falls Trail.): Goldenrod, Spotted Knapweed (quite a few), Daisy Fleabane [Sweet Scabious], Smooth False

Foxglove (quite a few), Birdsfoot Trefoil, Yellow Sweet Clover, Yarrow [Milfoil], Common St. Johnswort, Crown Vetch [Axseed], White Snakeroot, Spotted Touch-me-not [Jewelweed]

Middle of August

Railroad Run

Saratoga Springs, NY   Saratoga County

See Driving Directions, What to Expect, and Trail Information.

Late Season

Blacktop trail on right side: Spotted Knapweed (many in places), Black-eyed Susan (many in places), Daisy Fleabane [Sweet Scabious] (many), Yarrow [Milfoil], Blue Flax, Purple Coneflower, White Sweet Clover (near end of bloom), Day Lily (reddish-orange), Red Clover, Blanket Flower (quite a few - scattered), Rugosa Rose, Bladder Campion, Yellow Wood Sorrel, White Campion, Wild Carrot [Queen Anne's Lace, Bird's Nest] (many), Silvery Cinquefoil, Alfalfa [Lucerne], Bouncing Bet [Soapwort] (many in places), Yellow Sweet Clover (near end of bloom), Chicory, White Vervain, Goldenrod, Lance-leaved Coreopsis, Birdsfoot Trefoil, Common St. Johnswort, Cow [Tufted] Vetch, Deptford Pink, Pink Knotweed [Pinkweed], Rough-fruited [Sulphur] Cinquefoil, Common Evening Primrose, Rose Coreopsis [Pink Tickseed], Poppy, Bachelor's Button, Selfheal [Heal-all], Field Pennycress, Rabbit-foot Clover (quite a few)

Turn around at next road to go back on the other side: Many flowers seen before plus Common Mullein and Viper's Bugloss [Blueweed] (in mowed area).

Bog Meadow Brook Nature Trail

Saratoga Springs, NY   Saratoga County

*S*ee Driving Directions, What to Expect,
and Trail Information.

Late Season

By parking area: Purple Loosestrife, Canada Hawkweed, Wild Carrot [Queen Anne's Lace, Bird's Nest], Flat-topped Aster, Boneset [Thoroughwort], Birdsfoot Trefoil, Spotted Joe-Pye Weed, Hairy Willow Herb, Lady's Thumb, Purple-leaved Willow Herb, Dillen's Tick Trefoil, Spotted Touch-me-not [Jewelweed]

Nature Trail: Spotted Touch-me-not [Jewelweed], Hog Peanut (light purple), Purple Loosestrife, Red Clover, Dillen's Tick Trefoil, Yarrow [Milfoil], Selfheal [Heal-all] (near end of bloom), Spotted Joe-Pye Weed, Spiked Lobelia, Flat-topped Aster, Goldenrod, Daisy Fleabane [Sweet Scabious], Tall Meadow Rue (near end of bloom), White Sweet Clover, Yellow Wood Sorrel, Purple-stemmed Aster (beginning to bloom), Agrimony (near end of bloom), Deptford Pink, White Sweet Clover, Thimbleweed [Tall Anemone] (near end of bloom), Common St. Johnswort (near end of bloom), Common Evening Primrose, Wild Carrot [Queen Anne's Lace, Bird's Nest], Oxeye Daisy, Birdsfoot Trefoil, Bouncing Bet [Soapwort]

Bridge with handrail: White Snakeroot, Virgin's Bower, Tall [Green-headed] Coneflower, Violet (pale blue - one), Meadowsweet, Bittersweet Nightshade, Red-osier Dogwood (one), Naked-flowered Tick Trefoil

Turn around at 0.75 mile marker.

Plotter Kill Falls

Plotter Kill Nature Preserve
Rotterdam, NY   Schenectady County

See Driving Directions, What to Expect,
and Trail Information.

Late Season

Red trail (beginning on the boardwalk): Spiked Lobelia, Purple-leaved Willow Herb, Yellow Wood Sorrel, Motherwort, Selfheal [Heal-all], Nodding [Pale, Dock-leaved] Smartweed, White Avens (near end of bloom), White Wood Aster (quite a few), Heath Aster, Deptford Pink, Goldenrod, Daisy Fleabane [Sweet Scabious],Spotted Knapweed, Oxeye Daisy, Red Clover, Wild Carrot [Queen Anne's Lace, Bird's Nest], Yarrow [Milfoil], Schreber's Aster, Heart-leaved Aster (lavender), Silverrod (beginning to bloom)

After several small foot bridges: Zigzag (Broad-leaved] Goldenrod, Horse Balm [Richweed, Stoneroot], Hog Peanut

End of August

Shelving Rock Falls

Lake George Trail System
Fort Ann, NY   Washington County
See Driving Directions, What to Expect,
and Trail Information.

Late Season

Trail to the falls: White Sweet Clover, Goldenrod, Daisy Fleabane [Sweet Scabious], Red Clover, Wild Carrot [Queen Anne's Lace, Bird's Nest], Common Evening Primrose, Spotted Touch-me-not [Jewelweed], Common Burdock, White Wood Aster, Wood Nettle, Enchanter's Nightshade, Spiked Lobelia, Calico [Starved] Aster, Agrimony (near end of bloom), Cynthia, Arrow-leaved Tearthumb, Herb Robert

Harlem Valley Rail Trail

Millerton, NY   Dutchess County

See Driving Directions, What to Expect,
and Trail Information.

Late Season

Blacktop Trail: Yellow Wood Sorrel, Goldenrod, Dame's Violet [Dame's Rocket] (near end of bloom), Wild Balsam Apple [Wild Cucumber], Spotted Touch-me-not [Jewelweed] (many), Hedge Bindweed (white), Chicory (many), Wild Carrot [Queen Anne's Lace, Bird's Nest], Bouncing Bet [Soapwort] (near end of bloom), Purple Loosestrife, Red Clover, Deptford Pink, Daisy Fleabane [Sweet Scabious], Prickly Lettuce, Common Evening Primrose

First bridge: Spiked Lobelia, Pale Touch-me-not [Jewelweed], Boneset [Thoroughwort], Celandine, Pokeweed, Common St. Johnswort (near end of bloom)

Cross road and second bridge: White Snakeroot (many), White Wood Aster, Zigzag [Broad-leaved] Goldenrod, Nipplewort (quite a few)

Third bridge: Tall [Green-headed] Coneflower, Dittany, White Sweet Clover, Bladder Campion, Meadowsweet, Spotted Knapweed, Black Bindweed, Birdsfoot Trefoil, Common Sow Thistle, Lady's Thumb, Yellow Sweet Clover, Rough-fruited [Sulphur] Cinquefoil, Butter-and-eggs, Common Burdock, Field Hawkweed [King Devil], Trumpet [Coral] Honeysuckle (near end of bloom), White Campion

Past private driveway: Cynthia, Swamp Smartweed, Wild Bergamot, Wormseed [Treacle] Mustard, Horse Balm [Richweed, Stoneroot], White Avens

Turn around at building with greenhouse attached to it.

Railroad Run

Saratoga Springs, NY   Saratoga County

See Driving Directions, What to Expect,
and Trail Information.

Early Season

Blacktop trail on right side: Common Evening Primrose, Purple Coneflower, Day Lily, Rugosa Rose (near end of bloom), Cosmos, Spotted Knapweed (many), Blue Flax, Bladder Campion, Chicory, Red Clover, Wild Carrot [Queen

Anne's Lace, Bird's Nest], White Sweet Clover, Daisy Fleabane [Sweet Scabious], Bouncing Bet [Soapwort], Black-eyed Susan, Yellow Sweet Clover, White Campion, Common Mullein, Blanket Flower, Viper's Bugloss [Blueweed], Goldenrod, Butter-and-eggs, Cow [Tufted] Vetch, Yarrow [Milfoil] (pink)

Turn around at next road to go back on the other side.

Bog Meadow Brook Nature Trail

Saratoga Springs, NY   Saratoga County

See Driving Directions, What to Expect,
and Trail Information.

Early Season

Nature Trail: Spotted Touch-me-not [Jewelweed] (many), Goldenrod, Beggar Ticks [Sticktight], Flat-topped Aster, Purple-stemmed Aster, Lady's Thumb, Spotted Joe-Pye Weed, White Lettuce, Hog Peanut, Purple Loosestrife, Common Smartweed [Water Pepper], Water Horehound, Dillen's Tick Trefoil (near end of bloom), Canada Thistle, Yarrow [Milfoil] (near end of bloom), Daisy Fleabane [Sweet Scabious] (near end of bloom), Common Evening Primrose, Turtlehead, Deptford Pink, Birdsfoot Trefoil, Bouncing Bet [Soapwort], Oxeye Daisy, Agrimony

Over bridge with handrail: Wild Carrot [Queen Anne's Lace, Bird's Nest] (near end of bloom), White Sweet Clover, Meadowsweet (near end of bloom), Virgin's Bower

Turn around a short distance past the bridge.

Beginning of September

Plotter Kill Falls

Plotter Kill Nature and Historic Preserve
Rotterdam, NY   Schenectady County

See Driving Directions, What to Expect,
and Trail Information.

Late Season

Red Trail (beginning on the boardwalk):   Spiked Lobelia,
Calico [Starved] Aster, Purple-leaved Willow Herb, Yellow
Wood Sorrel, Goldenrod, Rough Cinquefoil, White Wood
Aster, Beggar Ticks [Sticktight], Bushy Aster, Wild Carrot
[Queen Anne's Lace, Bird's Nest], Silverrod, Heart-leaved
Aster

Down Yellow Trail to cascade and second falls: Spotted
Touch-me-not   [Jewelweed],   Zigzag   [Broad-leaved]
Goldenrod

Trail to top of the second falls: Indian Pipe [Corpse Plant],
Schreber's Aster

Back up to Red Trail and turn right to continue to third falls:
No new flowers

Harlem Valley Rail Trail

Millerton, NY   Dutchess County

See Driving Directions, What to Expect,
and Trail Information.

Late Season

Blacktop Trail: Goldenrod (many), Wild Balsam Apple [Wild Cucumber], Panicled Aster (beginning to bloom), Spotted Touch-me-not [Jewelweed] (many), Chicory, Wild Carrot [Queen Anne's Lace, Bird's Nest], Dittany, Pokeweed, White Snakeroot (many - scattered), Pale Touch-me-not [Jewelweed], Daisy Fleabane [Sweet Scabious]

Cross road and second bridge: Zigzag [Broad-leaved] Goldenrod, White Wood Aster, Nipplewort (near end of bloom)

Cross third bridge. Part of the area is mowed: Some flowers mentioned before plus Common Sow Thistle, Spotted Knapweed, Bouncing Bet [Soapwort] (white and pink), Butter-and-eggs, Beggar Ticks [Sticktight], Bladder Campion, Red Clover, Yellow Sweet Clover, Agrimony, Common Evening Primrose, Wild Basil, Yellow Wood Sorrel, Rough-fruited [Sulphur] Cinquefoil, Field Hawkweed [King Devil], Trumpet [Coral] Honeysuckle, Weigela (red - a few blooms)

Past private driveway: Field Sow Thistle, Lady's Thumb, Horse Balm [Richweed, Stoneroot], Herb Robert

Turn around at building with greenhouse attached to it.

Middle of September

Bog Meadow Brook Nature Trail

Saratoga Springs, NY   Saratoga County

See Driving Directions, What to Expect,
and Trail Information.

Late Season

Beside parking area: Purple-stemmed Aster, Goldenrod, Wild Carrot [Queen Anne's Lace, Bird's Nest], Birdsfoot Trefoil, Boneset [Thoroughwort] (near end of bloom), Flat-topped Aster, Lion's Foot [Gall-of-the-earth], Agrimony (near end of bloom), Spotted Joe-Pye Weed, Purple Loosestrife

Nature Trail (three foot area mowed on each side of trail): Flat-topped Aster (quite a few), Purple-stemmed Aster (beginning to bloom), Spotted Touch-me-not [Jewelweed], White Lettuce, Spotted Joe-Pye Weed (near end of bloom), Goldenrod, Red Clover, Yarrow [Milfoil], Calico [Starved] Aster (beginning to bloom), Yellow Wood Sorrel, Daisy Fleabane [Sweet Scabious], Deptford Pink (two)

Over bridge with handrail: Wild Carrot [Queen Anne's Lace, Bird's Nest], White Sweet Clover, Common Evening Primrose (one), Turtlehead (few), Purple Loosestrife, Meadowsweet (near end of bloom - one), Hog Peanut (very light purple), Boneset [Thoroughwort]

Turn around at 1.0 mile (1 MI) marker on tree to the right.

Railroad Run

Saratoga Springs, NY   Saratoga County

See Driving Directions, What to Expect,
and Trail Information.

Late Season

Blacktop trail on right side: White Sweet Clover (few),
Blanket Flower (many), Spotted Knapweed (many - near end
of bloom), Red Clover (quite a few), Rugosa Rose (rose),
Daisy Fleabane [Sweet Scabious] (quite a few), Bladder
Campion, Bouncing Bet [Soapwort] (mostly white, a few pink
- many), Wild Carrot [Queen Anne's Lace, Bird's Nest] (near
end of bloom), Common Evening Primrose (few), Black-eyed
Susan (many in one area), Butter-and-eggs, Purple
Coneflower, Yarrow [Milfoil], Goldenrod (many in places),
Rose of Sharon, Cow [Tufted] Vetch (quite a few in places),
Bachelor's Button, Pink Knotweed [Pinkweed], Rabbit-foot
Clover, Viper's Bugloss [Blueweed] (near end of bloom),
Yellow Wood Sorrel

Turn around at next road to go back on the other side: Some
flowers mentioned before plus Silvery Cinquefoil, Panicled
Aster, and New England Aster (rose-colored - one plant).

End of September

Harlem Valley Rail Trail

Millerton, NY   Dutchess County

See Driving Directions, What to Expect,
and Trail Information.

Late Season

<u>Blacktop trail (area beside trail recently mowed)</u>: Goldenrod, Panicled Aster, Dittany, Calico [Starved] Aster

<u>First bridge</u>: Spotted Touch-me-not [Jewelweed] (near end of bloom), Pale Touch-me-not [Jewelweed] (near end of bloom)

<u>Cross road and second bridge.</u>: White Snakeroot (many), Zigzag [Broad-leaved] Goldenrod (many), Blue-stemmed [Wreath] Goldenrod, Small White Aster (one), White Wood Aster

<u>Third bridge</u>: Prickly Lettuce, Common Sow Thistle, Bouncing Bet [Soapwort], Spotted Knapweed, Chicory, Swamp Smartweed, Bladder Campion, Yellow Wood Sorrel, Wild Carrot [Queen Anne's Lace, Bird's Nest] (near end of bloom), Beggar Ticks [Sticktight], Red Clover, Daisy Fleabane [Sweet Scabious], New England Aster, Dame's Violet [Dame's Rocket] (one), Deptford Pink (one), Black-eyed Susan (one), Wild Basil (near end of bloom), Common Evening Primrose, Butter-and-eggs, Trumpet [Coral] Honeysuckle

<u>Past private driveway</u>: Tall Rattlesnake Root [Gall-of-the-earth], Lady's Thumb

<u>Turn around at building with a greenhouse attached to it.</u>

Bog Meadow Brook Nature Trail

Saratoga Springs, NY   Saratoga County

See Driving Directions, What to Expect,
and Trail Information.

Late Season

By parking area: Goldenrod, Purple-stemmed Aster, Calico [Starved] Aster, Panicled Aster, Lady's Thumb, Spotted Joe-Pye Weed (near end of bloom), Wild Carrot [Queen Anne's Lace, Bird's Nest], Beggar Ticks [Sticktight], Flat-topped Aster, Turtlehead

Nature Trail: Purple-stemmed Aster (many), Goldenrod, Spotted Joe-Pye Weed (near end of bloom), Selfheal [Heal-all], Red Clover, Panicled Aster, Yarrow [Milfoil] (few), Calico [Starved] Aster, Yellow Wood Sorrel, Heart-leaved Aster (few), Thimbleweed [Tall Anemone] (one), Daisy Fleabane [Sweet Scabious], Rough Cinquefoil (one), Bouncing Bet [Soapwort] (few)

Bridge with handrail: Smooth Aster, Heath Aster, Common Evening Primrose (two), White Sweet Clover (one - near end of bloom), Many-flowered Aster, Turtlehead, Lowrie's Aster, Wild Carrot [Queen Anne's Lace, Bird's Nest] (few), Meadowsweet (one), White Lettuce, Tall Rattlesnake Root [Gall-of-the-earth]

Turn around at 1.0 mile (1 MI) marker on tree to the right.

Railroad Run

Saratoga Springs, NY   Saratoga County

See Driving Directions, What to Expect,
and Trail Information.

Late Season

Blacktop trail on right side (most of area mowed):   White
Sweet Clover, Yarrow [Milfoil], Blanket Flower, Purple
Coneflower, Rugosa Rose (rose), Spotted Knapweed, Daisy
Fleabane [Sweet Scabious] (quite a few - scattered), Red
Clover, Black-eyed Susan, Silvery Cinquefoil, Many-
flowered Aster (many), Panicled Aster (quite a few), Wild
Carrot [Queen Anne's Lace, Bird's Nest), Bladder Campion
(near end of bloom), Heath Aster, New England Aster
(purple), Rose of Sharon, Pink Knotweed [Pinkweed], Swamp
Smartweed, Hoary Alyssum, Bouncing Bet [Soapwort],
Butter-and-eggs, Bachelor's Button, Common Evening
Primrose, Yellow Wood Sorrel

Turn around at next road to go back on the other side: Some
flowers seen before plus New England Aster (rosy purple),
Meadowsweet (one), Common Mullein (one), Chicory (few)

Middle of October

Harlem Valley Rail Trail

Millerton, NY   Dutchess County

See Driving Directions, What to Expect,
and Trail Information.

Late Season

Blacktop trail: Smooth Aster, Bouncing Bet [Soapwort], Panicled Aster

First bridge: Goldenrod (few - near end of bloom)

Cross road and second bridge: Wild Carrot [Queen Anne's Lace, Bird's Nest] (few), Heart-leaved Aster (few), White Wood Aster (few)

Cross third bridge (area mowed):   Common Sow Thistle, Daisy Fleabane [Sweet Scabious] (few), Chicory (few), Spotted Knapweed (few), Calico [Starved] Aster (few - near end of bloom), Common Evening Primrose (one), Bladder Campion (one), Red Clover (one), White Snakeroot (most near end of bloom), Trumpet [Coral] Honeysuckle (most near end of bloom)

Past private driveway: Lady's Thumb (many), Herb Robert (one)

Turn around at building with greenhouse attached to it.

Railroad Run

Saratoga Springs, NY   Saratoga County

See Driving Directions, What to Expect,
and Trail Information.

Late Season

Blacktop trail on right side - (much mowed):   Bladder Campion (few), Blanket Flower, Daisy Fleabane [Sweet

Scabious], Rugosa Rose (near end of bloom), Spotted Knapweed, Chicory, Goldenrod (few - near end of bloom), Wild Carrot [Queen Anne's Lace, Bird's Nest] (few), Rose of Sharon, Butter-and-eggs, Hoary Alyssum (one), Pink Knotweed [Pinkweed] (one), Common Evening Primrose (two), Bachelor's Button (blue - few), Black-eyed Susan, Poppy (red - few), Red Clover

Turn around at next road to go back on other side.: Some flowers mentioned before plus New England Aster (purple), Chrysanthemum (white), Many-flowered Aster, Panicled Aster, Bouncing Bet [Soapwort] (few), Heart-leaved Aster (one)

Bog Meadow Brook Nature Trail

Saratoga Springs, NY   Saratoga County

See Driving Directions, What to Expect,
and Trail Information.

Late Season

By parking area: Wild Carrot [Queen Anne's Lace, Bird's Nest], Cattail, Purple-stemmed Aster, Goldenrod (near end of bloom), Panicled Aster (near end of bloom)

Nature Trail: Panicled Aster (one - near end of bloom), Calico [Starved] Aster (few - near end of bloom), Daisy Fleabane [Sweet Scabious] (few)

Bridge with handrail: Wild Carrot [Queen Anne's Lace, Bird's Nest] (one - near end of bloom), Red Clover (few),

White Sweet Clover (two), Goldenrod (few - near end of bloom), Yarrow [Milfoil] (few)

Turn around at 0.5 mile (0.5 MI) marker (very few flowers).

Vermont

End of May

D&H Rail Trail

Rupert, VT   Bennington County

See Driving Directions, What to Expect,
and Trail Information.

Late Season

Trail to right from Hebron Road: Marsh Marigold [Cowslip]
(many), Chokecherry (many), Apple tree, Golden Alexanders
(a few patches), Strawberry (many), Bird [Pin, Fire] Cherry,
Daffodil [Narcissus], Coltsfoot (near end of bloom), Common
Winter Cress [Yellow Rocket], Morrow's Honeysuckle
(beginning to bloom), Round-leaved Ragwort (beginning to
bloom - quite a few in spots), Common Cinquefoil, Hybrid of
Morrow's and Tartarian Honeysuckle (beginning to bloom)

Turn around where a short gravel road goes to a highway.
(Trail continues.*)*

Trail to left from Hebron Road: Common Winter Cress
[Yellow Rocket], Chokecherry (many), Strawberry (many),
Bird [Pin, Fire] Cherry

First bridge: Some flowers seen before plus Morrow's
Honeysuckle (beginning to bloom), Marsh Marigold
[Cowslip] (many), Apple tree

Turn around at second bridge.

Beginning of June

D&H Rail Trail

Rupert, VT   Bennington County

See Driving Directions, What to Expect,
and Trail Information.

Late Season

Trail to right from Hebron Road: Buttercup, Yellow
Goatsbeard, Dame's Violet [Dame's Rocket] (many at the
beginning of the trail and some other places), Field
Hawkweed [King Devil] (many), Marsh Marigold [Cowslip]
(near end of bloom), Red Clover, Apple tree (near end of
bloom), Common Blackberry, Morrow's Honeysuckle (near
end of bloom), Smaller Forget-me-not, Mouse Ear (many in
one place), Smaller Pussytoes, Common Cinquefoil,
Horseradish, Chokecherry, Alternate-leaved Dogwood,
Orange Hawkweed [Devil's Paintbrush] (many in one spot -
beginning to bloom), Lesser Stitchwort, Strawberry (few),
Great Angelica (beginning to bloom), Hybrid of Morrow's
and Tartarian Honeysuckle, Common Winter Cress [Yellow
Rocket], Wild Hydrangea (several), Hairy Rock Cress, Cow
[Tufted] Vetch (beginning to bloom), Silvery Cinquefoil
(one), Pink Azalea [Pinxter Flower] (in a yard), Bridal Wreath
(in a yard)

Past old Rupert Depot building: Blue-eyed Grass (one), Field
Peppergrass, Virginia Waterleaf (most white - a few light
purple), Yellow Wood Sorrel, Red-osier Dogwood, Tartarian
Honeysuckle

<u>Go past pond</u>: Oxeye Daisy (beginning to bloom), Round-leaved Ragwort (near end of bloom), Birdsfoot Trefoil, Golden Alexanders

<u>Turn around where a short, black gravel road connects trail with highway.   (Trail continues.)</u>

<u>Trail to left from Hebron Road</u>: Dame's Violet [Dame's Rocket], Common Winter Cress [Yellow Rocket], Bittersweet Nightshade, Blue-eyed Grass, Yellow Wood Sorrel, Field Hawkweed [King Devil] (many), Wild Hydrangea, Buttercup, Morrow's Honeysuckle (many)

<u>First bridge</u>: Red Clover, Birdsfoot Trefoil, Bladder Campion (beginning to bloom), Chokecherry, Common Blackberry, Mouse Ear (many), Wormseed [Treacle] Mustard, Yellow Goatsbeard, Strawberry, Field Peppergrass, Hybrid of Morrow's and Tartarian Honeysuckle, Tartarian Honeysuckle, Golden Alexanders, Tall Meadow Rue, Common Cinquefoil, Orange Hawkweed [Devil's Paintbrush], Marsh Marigold [Cowslip], Cow [Tufted] Vetch (beginning to bloom), Great Angelica (beginning to bloom)

<u>Turn around at second bridge</u>.

End of June

D&H Rail Trail

Rupert, VT   Bennington County

See Driving Directions, What to Expect,
and Trail Information.

Late Season

Trail to right from Hebron Road: Birdsfoot Trefoil (many), Red Clover, Wild Parsnip, Oxeye Daisy (many), Bladder Campion (quite a few), Dame's Violet [Dame's Rocket] (near end of bloom), Multiflora Rose, Buttercup, Deptford Pink (one), Field Hawkweed [King Devil] (many - some near end of bloom), Daisy Fleabane [Sweet Scabious], Mouse Ear (near end of bloom), Smaller Forget-me-not (many), Bittersweet Nightshade, Orange Hawkweed [Devil's Paintbrush] (some near end of bloom), Purple-flowering Raspberry, Viper's Bugloss [Blueweed], Great Angelica, Common Blackberry, Yarrow [Milfoil] (beginning to bloom), Yellow Wood Sorrel, Cow [Tufted] Vetch, Pineapple Weed, Rough-fruited [Sulphur] Cinquefoil, Tower Mustard (one), Rough Cinquefoil, Wormseed [Treacle] Mustard, Virginia Waterleaf (one - near end of bloom), Common Elder (quite a few), Meadowsweet (one - beginning to bloom), Panicled [Gray] Dogwood (quite a few), Round-leaved Ragwort (most finished), Common Cinquefoil, Lesser Stitchwort

Turn around where a short, black gravel road connects trail with highway.   (Trail continues.)

Trail to the left from Hebron Road: Wild Parsnip (quite a few), Multiflora Rose, Bittersweet Nightshade, Bladder Campion, Dame's Violet [Dame's Rocket], Daisy Fleabane [Sweet Scabious], Yellow Wood Sorrel, Red Clover, Pineapple Weed, Wormseed [Treacle] Mustard, Field Hawkweed [King Devil], Purple-flowering Raspberry, Oxeye Daisy, Smaller Forget-me-not

Over bridge: Cow [Tufted] Vetch, Birdsfoot Trefoil, Common Evening Primrose (one), Rough-fruited [Sulphur] Cinquefoil, Common Blackberry, Lesser Stitchwort, Mouse Ear (few), Yarrow [Milfoil] (beginning to bloom), Great Angelica,

Spreading Dogbane (quite a few in one area), Tall Meadow Rue (few), Larger Blue Flag Iris (quite a few in one area), Viper's Bugloss [Blueweed], Morrow's Honeysuckle (near end of bloom), Buttercup, Orange Hawkweed [Devil's Paintbrush] (most finished)

Turn around at second bridge.

Middle of July

Moss Glen Falls

Granville, VT   Addison County

See Driving Directions, What to Expect, and Trail Information.

Late Season

Flowers and wildflower plants along the boardwalk: Wild Parsnip, Buttercup, Helleborine (buds), Common Speedwell, Jack-in-the-pulpit [Indian Turnip] (leaves only), Hobblebush (leaves only), Common Wood Sorrel (leaves only), Canada Mayflower [Wild Lily-of-the-valley] (leaves and berries), Yellow Clintonia [Bluebead] (leaves only), Selfheal [Heal-all], Red Baneberry (leaves and berries), White Avens, Field Hawkweed [King Devil]

Texas Falls

Green Mountain National Forest
Hancock, VT   Addison County

See Driving Directions, What to Expect,
and Trail Information.

Late Season

<u>By the parking lot</u>: Buttercup

<u>Wildflower plants by the trail to the falls and waterfall
lookouts</u>:   Trillium (flowers finished), Jack-in-the-pulpit
[Indian Turnip] (leaves only), Hobblebush (leaves and
berries), Starflower (leaves only), Yellow Clintonia
[Bluebead] (leaves only), Canada Mayflower [Wild Lily-of-
the-valley] (leaves only), Sharp-leaved [Mountain, Whorled]
Aster (leaves only)

D&H Rail Trail

Rupert, VT   Bennington County

See Driving Directions, What to Expect,
and Trail Information.

Early Season

<u>Trail to right from Hebron Road</u>: Birdsfoot Trefoil (many),
Red Clover (quite a few), Wild Parsnip (many), Dame's Violet
[Dame's Rocket] (many), Deptford Pink, Rough-fruited
[Sulphur] Cinquefoil, Common Mullein, Common Evening
Primrose, Bladder Campion (many in spots - near end of
bloom), Common St. Johnswort, Bittersweet Nightshade
(many in spots), Smaller Forget-me-not (many), Larger Blue

Flag Iris, Purple-flowering Raspberry, Spreading Dogbane
(quite a few in spots), Yellow Wood Sorrel, Daisy Fleabane
[Sweet Scabious], Fringed Loosestrife, Canada Thistle,
Common Elder, Viper's Bugloss [Blueweed], Orange
Hawkweed [Devil's Paintbrush], Field Hawkweed [King
Devil], Bouncing Bet [Soapwort], Nipplewort

Cross farmyard road: Some flowers seen before plus Yarrow
[Milfoil] (near end of bloom), Rough Cinquefoil, Butter-and-
eggs, Red-osier Dogwood, Tall Meadow Rue, Oxeye Daisy
(many in spots), Cow [Tufted] Vetch (many in spots), White
Sweet Clover (many in spots), Crown Vetch [Axseed] (many
in one place)

Past building that says "Rupert Depot": Some flowers seen
before plus Meadowsweet, Goldenrod (beginning to bloom),
Common Milkweed, Swamp Rose (many in spots), Wild
Carrot [Queen Anne's Lace, Bird's Nest] (beginning to
bloom), Common Cattail, Spotted Joe-Pye Weed (beginning
to bloom)

Turn around where a short, black gravel road connects trail
with highway. (Trail continues.)

Trail to left from Hebron Road: Wild Parsnip, Bittersweet
Nightshade, Common St. Johnswort, Purple-flowering
Raspberry, Dame's Violet [Dame's Rocket], Field Hawkweed
[King Devil], Bouncing Bet [Soapwort], Oxeye Daisy (many
in spots), Rough-fruited [Sulphur] Cinquefoil, Day Lily
(orange - many along the edge of the trail), Cow [Tufted]
Vetch, Butter-and-eggs, Bladder Campion, Daisy Fleabane
[Sweet Scabious], Common Mullein, Bull Thistle, Staghorn
Sumac, Deptford Pink, Common Evening Primrose (many in
one spot), Common Milkweed, Canada Thistle (beginning to
bloom), Spotted Knapweed (beginning to bloom), Common
Elder, Purple Milkweed, Yarrow [Milfoil], Viper's Bugloss

[Blueweed], Fireweed [Great Willow Herb] (beginning to bloom), Hedge Bindweed (white), Buttercup, Meadowsweet, Spreading Dogbane (many in spots), Common Cattail, Common Hedge Nettle (small), Hemp Nettle (white - small), Fringed Loosestrife (many in one spot), Orange Hawkweed [Devil's Paintbrush] (near end of bloom), Tall Meadow Rue, Silky Dogwood

Turn around at second bridge.

End of July

D&H Rail Trail

Rupert, VT   Bennington County

See Driving Directions, What to Expect,
and Trail Information.

Early Season

Trail to right from Hebron Road: Bouncing Bet [Soapwort] (many - white and pink), Red Clover (quite a few), Dame's Violet [Dame's Rocket] (near end of bloom), Wild Parsnip (many), Yarrow [Milfoil], Common Evening Primrose, Birdsfoot Trefoil (many), Bladder Campion (near end of bloom), Bittersweet Nightshade, Purple-flowering Raspberry (quite a few), Spreading Dogbane (quite a few), Smaller Forget-me-not (many), White Campion, Deptford Pink, Common St. Johnswort, Rough-fruited [Sulphur] Cinquefoil, Daisy Fleabane [Sweet Scabious] (many in places), Canada Thistle (many in places), Viper's Bugloss [Blueweed], Spotted Joe-Pye Weed (beginning to bloom - many in places), Spotted

Touch-me-not [Jewelweed] (beginning to bloom), Butter-and-eggs, Orange Hawkweed [Devil's Paintbrush], Rough Cinquefoil, Oxeye Daisy, Yarrow [Milfoil], Wild Basil, Meadowsweet (many), Cow [Tufted] Vetch, White Sweet Clover (many in spots), Crown Vetch [Axseed], Wild Bergamot, Spotted Knapweed, Field Hawkweed [King Devil] (one), Cardinal Flower (quite a few), Swamp Milkweed, Tall Meadow Rue, Common Elder, Blue Vervain, Common Milkweed, Goldenrod (beginning to bloom)

Flowers in and beside pond: Water Smartweed, Swamp Rose, Common Cattail, Steeplebush [Hardhack]

Turn around where a short black gravel road connects trail with highway. (Trail continues.)

Beginning of August

D&H Rail Trail

Rupert, VT   Bennington County

See Driving Directions, What to Expect,
and Trail Information.

Early Season

Trail to right from Hebron Road: Birdsfoot Trefoil (many), Bouncing Bet [Soapwort] (many in spots), Common Evening Primrose, Red Clover (many), Goldenrod, Yarrow [Milfoil], Bittersweet Nightshade, Dame's Violet [Dame's Rocket] (near end of bloom), Butter-and-eggs, Spotted Touch-me-not [Jewelweed], Peppermint, Spotted Joe-Pye Weed (many), Smaller Forget-me-not (many in spots), Spreading Dogbane,

Purple-flowering Raspberry, Spotted Knapweed, Common St. Johnswort, Deptford Pink (few), Canada Thistle, Meadowsweet (many), Viper's Bugloss [Blueweed], Mouse Ear, Schreber's Aster, Yellow Wood Sorrel, Wild Basil

Trail continues (area mowed): Daisy Fleabane [Sweet Scabious], Oxeye Daisy (few), Bladder Campion, White Sweet Clover (few), Wild Bergamot, Yarrow [Milfoil] (near end of bloom), Wild Carrot [Queen Anne's Lace, Bird's Nest], Yellow Goatsbeard, Virgin's Bower, Pale Touch-me-not [Jewelweed], Hedge Bindweed (pink), Cow [Tufted] Vetch, Common Burdock, Cardinal Flower, Tall Nettle, Boneset [Thoroughwort], Shrubby Cinquefoil, Blue Vervain

Trail continues past pond (area not mowed): Water Smartweed, Steeplebush [Hardhack] (many in some areas), Spiked Lobelia, Common Milkweed, Flat-topped Aster, Fringed Loosestrife, Dittany

Turn around where a short black gravel road connects trail with highway. (Trail continues.)

Trail to left from Hebron Road: Bouncing Bet [Soapwort] (many - near end of bloom), Bittersweet Nightshade, Spotted Touch-me-not [Jewelweed], Wild Parsnip (near end of bloom), Common Evening Primrose (quite a few), Goldenrod (many in spots), Wild Balsam Apple [Wild Cucumber], Rabbit-foot Clover, Spotted Joe-Pye Weed (many), Purple-flowering Raspberry, Pale Touch-me-not [Jewelweed], Hedge Bindweed (white), Smaller Forget-me-not, Oxeye Daisy (few), Red Clover, Dame's Violet [Dame's Rocket] (near end of bloom), Wild Basil (pink, lilac), Steeplebush [Hardhack], Common Burdock, Common St. Johnswort, Blue Vervain, Yarrow [Milfoil] (near end of bloom), Spotted Knapweed (many in spots), Butter-and-eggs, Bull Thistle, Daisy Fleabane [Sweet Scabious], Bladder Campion (near end of bloom), Deptford Pink (few), Common Mullein, Wild Bergamot, Viper's Bugloss [Blueweed] (near end of bloom), Canada Thistle (near end of bloom), Wild Carrot [Queen Anne's Lace, Bird's Nest] (few), Virgin's Bower, Common Elder (near end of bloom), Fireweed [Great Willow Herb] (few), Common Milkweed, Meadowsweet (quite a few), Spreading Dogbane (many in one area), Boneset [Thoroughwort], Cattail (many), Dittany, Schreber's Aster, Rough-fruited [Sulphur] Cinquefoil, Hemp Nettle, Yellow Wood Sorrel, White Sweet Clover, Field Hawkweed [King Devil] (one), Mouse Ear, Spiked Lobelia (one)

Turn around at second bridge.

End of August

D&H Rail Trail

Rupert, VT   Bennington County

See Driving Directions, What to Expect,
and Trail Information.

Early Season

Trail to right of Hebron Road (area mowed): Bouncing Bet [Soapwort] (many), Birdsfoot Trefoil (many), Goldenrod (many), Red Clover, Common Evening Primrose (near end of bloom), Spotted Touch-me-not [Jewelweed] (many), Bladder Campion (most near end of bloom), Spotted Joe-Pye Weed (many - some near end of bloom), Turtlehead (few), Smaller Forget-me-not (many), Purple-stemmed Aster, Spreading Dogbane, Bittersweet Nightshade, Wild Basil, Peppermint (many), Purple-flowering Raspberry, Chicory (few), Canada

Thistle (near end of bloom), Viper's Bugloss [Blueweed], Pale Touch-me-not [Jewelweed] (one), Mouse Ear (quite a few in one area), Field Hawkweed [King Devil] (few), Butter-and-eggs (near end of bloom), Schreber's Aster, Meadowsweet (most are finished), White Sweet Clover (one), Orange Hawkweed [Devil's Paintbrush] (one), Daisy Fleabane [Sweet Scabious] (few), Wild Bergamot, Yellow Goatsbeard (one), Blue Curls, Yellow Wood Sorrel, Wild Chamomile, White Wood Aster (one), Oxeye Daisy (few), Tall Nettle, Deptford Pink (few), Cardinal Flower (near end of bloom), Boneset [Thoroughwort], Wild Carrot [Queen Anne's Lace, Bird's Nest]

Past pond: Swamp Milkweed (one), Nodding [Pale, Dock-leaved] Smartweed, Water Smartweed (quite a few), Cow [Tufted] Vetch, Cattail, Common Mullein (most finished), Steeplebush [Hardhack] (most finished), Flat-topped Aster, Spotted Knapweed (most finished)

Turn around where a short, black gravel road connects trail with highway. (Trail continues)

Trail to left of Hebron Road: Bouncing Bet [Soapwort] (many), Bittersweet Nightshade, Spotted Touch-me-not [Jewelweed], Pale Touch-me-not [Jewelweed] (few), Spotted Joe-Pye Weed (many), Virgin's Bower (quite a few), Goldenrod (many in the distance), Common Evening Primrose (many), Blue Vervain (one), Wild Balsam Apple [Wild Cucumber], Purple-flowering Raspberry, Red Clover, Rabbit-foot Clover, Common Mullein (many), Spotted Knapweed, Bull Thistle, Daisy Fleabane [Sweet Scabious], Bladder Campion (near end of bloom), Butter-and-eggs, Oxeye Daisy, Dittany, Deptford Pink (one), Wild Bergamot (near end of bloom), Meadowsweet, (near end of bloom), Spotted St. Johnswort (near end of bloom), Viper's Bugloss [Blueweed] (near end of bloom), Wild Carrot [Queen Anne's

Lace, Bird's Nest], Fireweed [Great Willow Herb], (few), Boneset [Thoroughwort], Hedge Bindweed, Large-leaved Aster (many in one place), Steeplebush [Hardhack] (near end of bloom), Spreading Dogbane, Cattail (many), Purple-stemmed Aster (one), Hemp Nettle (white with purple stripes - few), Field Hawkweed [King Devil] (one)

<u>Turn around at second bridge.</u>

Beginning of September

D&H Rail Trail

Rupert, VT   Bennington County

See Driving Directions, What to Expect,
and Trail Information.

Late Season

<u>Trail to the right of Hebron Road</u>: Birdsfoot Trefoil (many - scattered), Bouncing Bet [Soapwort] (white and pink - quite a few), Purple-stemmed Aster (many in places), Chicory (few), Spotted Touch-me-not [Jewelweed] (many), Wild Balsam Apple [Wild Cucumber], Red Clover, Goldenrod (many - some near end of bloom), Common Evening Primrose, Bladder Campion (quite a few), Yellow Wood Sorrel (many), Peppermint, Spotted Joe-Pye Weed (many in spots), Deptford Pink (few), Field Hawkweed [King Devil] (few), Viper's Bugloss [Blueweed], Purple-flowering Raspberry (near end of bloom), Mouse Ear, Bittersweet Nightshade, Butter-and-eggs (quite a few), Calico [Starved] Aster, Smaller Forget-me-not, Daisy Fleabane [Sweet Scabious], Nipplewort, Rough-fruited [Sulphur] Cinquefoil, Common Mullein (few), Rough

Cinquefoil, Schreber's Aster (near end of bloom), Orange Hawkweed [Devil's Paintbrush] (few), Common St. Johnswort (near end of bloom), Oxeye Daisy (one), White Sweet Clover, White Snakeroot, Tall Nettle, Pale Touch-me-not [Jewelweed], Wild Bergamot (one), Cardinal Flower (near end of bloom), Turtlehead (few), Yarrow [Milfoil] (few - near end of bloom), Sweet Everlasting [Catfoot] (one), Meadowsweet (near end of bloom), Pink Knotweed [Pinkweed] (one), Boneset [Thoroughwort], Wild Carrot [Queen Anne's Lace, Bird's Nest], Water Smartweed, Nodding Ladies' Tresses, Cow [Tufted] Vetch, Dittany, Heath Aster, Flat-topped Aster, Spotted Knapweed (near end of bloom), Steeplebush (one), Purple-leaved Willow Herb, Red Clover (with white bloom)

Turn around when a short, black gravel road connects trail with highway. (Trail continues.)

Trail to left of Hebron Road: Bouncing Bet [Soapwort] (white and pink - quite a few), Spotted Touch-me-not [Jewelweed] (many), Wild Carrot [Queen Anne's Lace, Bird's Nest], Daisy Fleabane [Sweet Scabious], Common St. Johnswort (near end of bloom), Common Evening Primrose (quite a few), Pale Touch-me-not [Jewelweed], Wild Balsam Apple [Wild Cucumber], Bladder Campion, Rough Cinquefoil, Goldenrod (many), Purple-flowering Raspberry

First bridge: Purple Loosestrife (one), Chicory (one), White Sweet Clover, Yellow Wood Sorrel (quite a few), Birdsfoot Trefoil, Spotted Joe-Pye Weed (many - some near end of bloom), Hedge Bindweed (white - many in spots), Butter-and-eggs (quite a few), Spotted Knapweed, Common Mullein, Field Hawkweed [King Devil], Mouse Ear, Dittany, Red Clover, Bittersweet Nightshade, Sweet Everlasting [Catfoot] (one), Purple-stemmed Aster (many in spots), Common Cattail (many in spots), Meadowsweet, Large-leaved Aster,

Boneset [Thoroughwort], Rough-fruited [Sulphur] Cinquefoil, Flat-topped Aster, Steeplebush [Hardhack] (one - near end of bloom), Viper's Bugloss [Blueweed] (many - near end of bloom), Wild Basil, White Wood Aster

Turn around at second bridge.

Middle of September

D&H Rail Trail

Rupert, VT   Bennington County

See Driving Directions, What to Expect, and Trail Information.

Late Season

Trail to right of Hebron Road: Red Clover (many), Bouncing Bet [Soapwort] (quite a few), Panicled Aster, Purple-stemmed Aster (many in spots), Birdsfoot Trefoil (few), Common Evening Primrose, Bladder Campion, Spotted Touch-me-not [Jewelweed], Goldenrod, Spotted Joe-Pye Weed (most near end of bloom), Viper's Bugloss [Blueweed], Purple-flowering Raspberry, Calico [Starved] Aster, Butter-and-eggs, Nipplewort, Common Cattail, Field Hawkweed [King Devil] (few), Daisy Fleabane [Sweet Scabious], Large-leaved Aster (near end of bloom), Orange Hawkweed [Devil's Paintbrush], New England Aster (few), Oxeye Daisy, Yellow Goatsbeard, White Sweet Clover (few)

Past Rupert Depot: White Snakeroot, Yarrow [Milfoil], Spiny-leaved Sow Thistle (one), Sweet Everlasting (one), Tall Nettle

By pond: Pink Knotweed [Pinkweed], Water Smartweed, Nodding Ladies' Tresses (quite a few), Boneset [Thoroughwort] (near end of bloom), Common Mullein, Mouse Ear, Heath Aster, Dittany (near end of bloom), Meadowsweet (near end of bloom), Spotted Knapweed (near end of bloom), Wild Carrot [Queen Anne's Lace, Bird's Nest], Flat-topped Aster, Larger Bur Marigold

Turn around where a short, black gravel road connects trail with highway. Trail continues.)

Trail to left of Hebron Road: Bouncing Bet [Soapwort] (light pink and white - quite a few), Wild Carrot [Queen Anne's Lace, Bird's Nest], Common Evening Primrose, Panicled Aster, Daisy Fleabane [Sweet Scabious], Spotted Touch-me-not [Jewelweed] (many), Common St. Johnswort (few - near end of bloom), Goldenrod (many), Common Mullein, Pale Touch-me-not [Jewelweed]

First bridge: Purple-stemmed Aster (quite a few - scattered), Purple Loosestrife (one), Spotted Knapweed (near end of bloom), Chicory (few), Red Clover, White Sweet Clover (few), Heart-leaved Aster (few), Bladder Campion, Spotted Joe-Pye Weed (many - near end of bloom), Yellow Wood Sorrel, Hedge Bindweed (white), Mouse Ear, Butter-and-eggs, Tall Nettle (one), Dittany, Viper's Bugloss [Blueweed], Field Hawkweed [King Devil], Sweet Everlasting [Catfoot], Meadowsweet (near end of bloom), Common Cattail (many in two spots), Hairy Willow Herb (many near Cattails), Yarrow [Milfoil] (one - near end of bloom), Orange Hawkweed [Devil's Paintbrush] (one), Thin-leaved Sunflower

Turn around at second bridge.

Beginning of October

D&H Rail Trail

Rupert, VT   Bennington County

See Driving Directions, What to Expect,
and Trail Information.

Early Season

Trail to right of Hebron Road: Bouncing Bet [Soapwort]
(quite a few), Panicled Aster, Red Clover (quite a few),
Goldenrod (near end of bloom), Bittersweet Nightshade,
Deptford Pink (one), Common Evening Primrose (few),
Viper's Bugloss [Blueweed] (quite a few), Mouse Ear (one),
Purple-stemmed Aster (few), Butter-and-eggs (many), Heart-
leaved Aster, Yellow Wood Sorrel, Bladder Campion (many),
Orange Hawkweed [Devil's Paintbrush] (one), Birdsfoot
Trefoil (few), Wild Parsnip (few), Daisy Fleabane [Sweet
Scabious], White Sweet Clover (few), Oxeye Daisy (few),
White Campion, Yellow Goatsbeard (few), Wild Carrot
[Queen Anne's Lace, Bird's Nest] (few), Canada Hawkweed
(one), White Wood Aster (one), White Snakeroot (few),
Lowrie's Aster (few), Water Smartweed (few), Field
Hawkweed [King Devil] (one), Heath Aster (few), Spotted
Knapweed (few), Flat-topped Aster (near end of bloom), New
England Aster (few), Cattail

Turn around where a black, gravel road connects trail with
highway. (Trail continues.)

Trail to left of Hebron Road: Bouncing Bet [Soapwort] (white
and pink - quite a few), Panicled Aster, Goldenrod (near end
of bloom), Yellow Wood Sorrel (few), Red Clover (many in
one spot), Bladder Campion, Common Mullein (few),

Common Evening Primrose (near end of bloom), Spotted Knapweed (near end of bloom), Wild Carrot [Queen Anne's Lace, Bird's Nest] (few), Butter-and-eggs, Daisy Fleabane [Sweet Scabious] (two), Common St. Johnswort (one - near end of bloom), Field Hawkweed [King Devil] (few), Cattail (near end of bloom), Purple-stemmed Aster (few), Viper's Bugloss [Blueweed]

Turn around at second bridge.

End of October

D&H Rail Trail

Rupert, VT   Bennington County

See Driving Directions, What to Expect, and Trail Information.

Early Season

Trail to right of Hebron Road: Goldenrod (near end of bloom), Daisy Fleabane [Sweet Scabious] (near end of bloom), Wild Parsnip, Viper's Bugloss [Blueweed] (near end of bloom)

Turn around where a short, black gravel road connects trail with highway. (Trail continues.)

Trail to left of Hebron Road: Goldenrod (near end of bloom), Common Mullein, Bouncing Bet [Soapwort] (near end of bloom), Butter-and-eggs

Turn around at second bridge.

SCIENTIFIC-COMMON NAME EQUIVALENTS

Acer pensylvanicum - Maple, Striped
Achillea millefolium - Milfoil
Achillea millefolium - Yarrow
Aconitum uncinatum - Monkshood, Wild
Actaea - Baneberry
Actaea pachypoda - Baneberry, White
Actaea pachypoda - Doll's Eyes
Actaea rubra - Baneberry, Red
Adlumia fungosa - Allegheny Vine
Adlumia fungosa - Fumitory, Climbing
Adlumia fungosa - Mountain Fringe
Agrimonia gryposepala - Agrimony
Ajuga - Bugle
Aletris farinosa - Colicroot
Alliaria officinalis - Mustard, Garlic
Allium cernuum - Onion, Nodding Wild
Allium tricoccum - Leek, Wild
Allium tricoccum - Ramps
Amelanchier arborea - Shadbush, Common
Amelanchier laevis - Shadbush, Smooth
Amianthium muscaetoxicum - Fly Poison
Amphicarpa bracteata - Hog Peanut
Amsonia tabernaemontana -Bluestar
Anaphalis margaritacea - Everlasting, Pearly
Anemone quinquefolia - Anemone, Wood
Anemone virginiana - Anemone, Tall
Anemone virginiana - Thimbleweed
Anemonella thalictroides - Anemone, Rue
Angelica atropurpurea - Angelica, Great
Antennaria neglecta - Pussytoes, Field
Antennaria parlinii - Pussytoes, Smooth
Antennaria plantaginifolia - Pussytoes, Plantain-leaved
Antennaria neodioica - Pussytoes, Smaller
Apocynum cannabinum - Hemp, Indian

Apocynun androsa emifolium - Dogbane, Spreading
Aquilegia canadensis - Columbine, Wild
Arabis blepharophylla - Rock Cress, Pink
Arabis glabra - Mustard, Tower
Arabis hirsuta - Rock Cress, Hairy
Aralia hispida - Sarsaparilla, Bristly
Aralia nudicaulis - Sarsaparilla, Wild
Arctium minus - Burdock, Common
Arenaria lateriflora - Sandwort, Blunt-leaved
Arenaria lateriflora - Sandwort, Grove
Arisaema - Jack-in-the-pulpit
Arisaema atrorubens - Indian Turnip
Armoracia lapathifolia - Horseradish
Asarum canadense - Ginger, Wild
Asclepias incarnata - Milkweed, Swamp
Asclepias purpurascens - Milkweed, Purple
Asclepias syriaca - Milkweed, Common
Asclepias tuberosa - Butterfly Weed
Asclepias tuberosa - Pleurisy Root
Aster acuminatus - Aster, Mountain
Aster acuminatus - Aster, Sharp-leaved
Aster acuminatus - Aster, Whorled
Aster cordifolius - Aster, Heart-leaved
Aster divaricatus - Aster, White Wood
Aster divaricatus - Aster, Wood
Aster dumosus - Aster, Bushy
Aster ericoides - Aster, Many-flowered
Aster laevis - Aster, Smooth
Aster lateriflorus - Aster, Starved
Aster lateriflorus - Aster, Calico
Aster linariifolius - Aster, Bristly
Aster linariifolius - Aster, Stiff
Aster lowrieanus - Aster, Lowrie's
Aster macrophyllus - Aster, Large-leaved
Aster nemoralis - Aster, Bog
Aster novae-angliae - Aster, New England

Aster novi-belgii - Aster, New York
Aster oblongifolius - Aster, Aromatic
Aster patens - Aster, Late Purple
Aster patens - Aster, Spreading
Aster pilosus - Aster, Heath
Aster ptarmicoides - Aster, Upland
Aster ptarmicoides - Aster, Upland White
Aster puniceus - Aster, Purple-stemmed
Aster schreberi - Aster, Schreber's
Aster simplex - Aster, Panicled
Aster spectabilis - Aster, Showy
Aster umbellatus - Aster, Flat-topped
Aster undulatus - Aster, Wavy-leaved
Aster vimineus - Aster, Small White
Barbarea vulgaris - Rocket, Yellow
Barbarea vulgaris - Winter Cress, Common
Berteroa - Alyssum, Hoary
Bidens frondosa - Beggar Ticks
Bidens frondosa - Sticktight
Bidens laevis - Bur Marigold, Larger
Blephilia hirsuta - Wood Mint, Hairy
Callirhoe digitata - Mallow, Poppy
Callirhoe involucrata - Mallow, Poppy
Callirhoe triangulata - Mallow, Poppy
Calluna vulgaris - Heather
Calluna vulgaris - Ling
Calopogon pulchellus - Grass Pink
Calopogon pulchellus - Grass Pink Orchid
Caltha palustris - Cowslip
Caltha palustris - Marigold, Marsh
Campanula rotundifolia - Bluebell
Campanula rotundifolia - Harebell
Capsella bursa-pastoris - Shepherd's Purse
Cardamine pratenses - Cuckooflower
Caulophyllum thalictroides - Cohosh, Blue
Centaurea cyanus - Bachelor's Button

Centaurea maculosa - Knapweed, Spotted
Cerastium vulgatum - Chickweed, Mouse-ear
Cercis - Redbud
Chamaedaphne calyculata - Leatherleaf
Chamaelinium luteum - Blazing Star
Chamaelirium luteum - Devil's Bit
Chamaelirium luteum - Fairy Wand
Chelidonium majus - Celandine
Chelone glabra - Turtlehead
Chelone lyoni - Turtlehead, Pink
Chemaphila maculata - Wintergreen, Striped
Chimaphila maculata - Wintergreen, Spotted
Chrysanthemum - Chrysanthemum
Chrysanthemum leucanthemum - Daisy, Oxeye
Chrysogonum virginianum - Golden Star
Chrysopsis fakcata - Aster, Cape Golden
Chrysopsis falcata - Aster, Sickle-leaved Golden
Chrysopsis mariana - Aster, Broad-leaved Golden
Chrysopsis mariana - Aster, Maryland Golden
Chrysopsis villosa - Aster, Prairie Golden
Cichorium intybus - Chicory
Cimicifuga racemosa - Cohosh, Black
Cimicifuga racemosa - Snakeroot, Black
Circaea quadrisulcata - Nightshade, Enchanter's
Cirsium arvense - Thistle, Canada
Cirsium vulgare - Thistle, Bull
Claytonia caroliniana - Spring Beauty, Carolina
Claytonia virginica - Spring Beauty
Clematis - Clematis
Clematis virginiana - Virgin's Bower
Clethra alnifolia - Pepperbush, Sweet
Clintonia borealis - Bluebead
Clintonia borealis - Clintonia, Yellow
Collinsonia canadensis - Horse Balm
Collinsonia canadensis - Richweed
Collinsonia canadensis - Stoneroot

Conioselinum chinese - Parsley, Hemlock
Convolvulus sepium - Bindweed, Hedge
Coptis groenlandica - Goldthread
Coreopsis ariculata - Coreopsis, Eared
Coreopsis lancelata - Coreopsis, Lance-leaved
Coreopsis rosea - Coreopsis, Rose
Coreopsis rosea - Tickseed, Pink
Cornus alternifolia - Dogwood, Alternate-leaved
Cornus amomum - Dogwood, Silky
Cornus florida - Dogwood, Flowering
Cornus kousa - Dogwood, Japanese
Cornus kousa - Dogwood, Korean
Cornus kousa - Dogwood, Kousa
Cornus racemosa - Dogwood, Gray
Cornus racemosa - Dogwood, Panicled
Cornus solonifera - Dogwood, Red-osier
Coronilla varia - Axseed
Coronilla varia - Vetch, Crown
Corydalis sempervirens - Corydalis, Pink
Corydalis sempervirens - Corydalis, Pale
Cosmos - Cosmos
Crataegus - Hawthorn
Crepis capillaris - Hawksbeard, Smooth
Cryptotaenia canadensis - Honewort
Cunila origanoides - Dittany
Cypripedium acaule - Lady's Slipper, Pink
Cypripedium acaule - Moccasin Flower
Cypripedium calceolus pubescens - Lady's Slipper, Larger Yellow
Cypripedium parviflorum - Lady's Slipper, Smaller Yellow
Cardamine pratenses - Lady's Smock
Daucus carota - Bird's Nest
Daucus carota - Carrot, Wild
Daucus carota - Queen Anne's Lace
Dentaria diphylla - Crinkleroot
Dentaria diphylla - Toothwort

Desmodium canadense - Tick Trefoil, Showy
Desmodium glabellum - Tick Trefoil, Dillen's
Desmodium nudiflorum - Tick Trefoil, Naked-flowered
Desmodium paniculatum - Tick Trefoil, Panicled
Dianthus - Pink
Dianthus armeria - Pink, Deptford
Dianthus barbatus - Sweet William
Dianthus deltoides - Pink, Maiden
Dicentra - Dutchman's Breeches
Dicentra cucullaria - Squirrel Corn
Dicentra eximia - Bleeding Heart, Wild
Diervilla lonicera - Honeysuckle, Bush
Diphylleie cymosa - Umbrella Leaf
Dodecatheon amethystinum - Shooting Star, Jewel
Dodecatheon meadia - Shooting Star
Drosera rotundifolia - Sundew, Round-leaved
Echinacea purpurea - Coneflower, Purple
Echinocystis lobata - Balsam Apple, Wild
Echinocystis lobata - Cucumber, Wild
Echium vulgare - Blueweed
Echium vulgare - Bugloss, Viper's
Elaeagnus augustifolia - Russian-olive shrub
Epigaea regens - Arbutus, Trailing
Epigaea repens - Mayflower
Epilobium augustifolium - Fireweed
Epilobium augustifolium - Willow Herb, Great
Epilobium coloratum - Willow Herb, Purple-leaved
Anemone quinquefolia - Windflower
Epilobium hirsutum - Willow Herb, Hairy
Epipactis helleborine - Helleborine
Erigeron annuus - Scabious, Sweet
Erigeron annuus - Fleabane, Daisy
Erigeron canadensis - Horseweed
Erigeron philadelphicus - Fleabane, Common
Erigeron philadelphicus - Fleabane, Philadelphia
Erigeron pulchellus - Robin's Plantain

Erigeron strigosus - Fleabane, Lesser Daisy
Erthronium albidum - Adder's Tongue, White
Erthronium americanum - Adder's Tongue, Yellow
Erysimum cheiranthoides - Mustard, Treacle
Erysimum cheiranthoides - Mustard, Wormseed
Erythronium albidum - Lily, White Trout
Erythronium americanum - Lily, Trout
Euonymus atropurpureus - Burning Bush
Euonymus atropurpureus - Wahoo
Eupatorium coelestinum - Mistflower
Eupatorium maculatum - Joe-Pye Weed, Spotted
Eupatorium perfoliatum - Boneset
Eupatorium perfoliatum - Thoroughwort
Eupatorium rotundifolium - Boneset, Round-leaved
Eupatorium rugosum - Snakeroot, White
Euphorbia cyparissias - Spurge, Cypress
Fragaria - Strawberry
Fragaria virginiana - Strawberry, Wild
Gaillardia - Blanket Flower
Galeopsis tetrahit - Nettle, Hemp
Galium mollugo - Madder, Wild
Galium triflorum - Bedstraw, Sweet-scented
Gentiana autumnalis - Gentian, Pine Barren
Gentiana clausa - Gentian, Bottle
Gentiana clausa - Gentian, Closed
Gentiana crinita - Gentian, Fringed
Gentiana linearis - Gentian, Narrow-leaved
Gentiana villosa - Gentian, Striped
Gentiana villosa - Snakeroot, Sampson's
Geranium maculatum - Cranesbill, Spotted
Geranium maculatum - Geranium, Wild
Geranium robertianum - Herb Robert
Gerardia purpurea - Gerardia, Purple
Gerdardia flava - False Foxglove, Smooth
Geum aleppicum - Avens, Yellow
Geum canadens - Avens, White

Geum rivale - Avens, Purple
Geum rivale - Avens, Water
Geum triflorum - Prairie Smoke
Geum virginianum - Avens, Cream-colored
Gillenia - Bowman's Root
Gillenia - Indian Physic
Glechoma hederacea - Gill-over-the-ground
Glechoma hederacea - Ground Ivy
Gnaphalium obtusifolium - Catfoot
Gnaphalium obtusifolium - Everlasting, Sweet
Goodyera pubescens - Rattlesnake Plantain, Downy
Habenaria ciliaris - Orchid, Yellow Fringed
Habenaria ciliaris - Orchis Yellow Fringed
Habenaria psycodes - Orchis, Smaller Purple Fringed
Helenium autumnale - Sneezeweed
Helianthus decapetalus - Sunflower, Thin-leaved
Helianthus strumosus - Sunflower, Pale-leaved
Helonias bullata - Pink, Swamp
Helonias bullata - Swamp Hyacinth
Hemerocallis fulva - Lily, Day
Hepatica acutiloba - Hepatica, Sharp-lobed
Hepatica americana - Hepatica, Round-lobed
Hepatica americana - Liverleaf
Hesperis matronalis - Violet, Dame's
Hesperis matronalis - Rocket, Dame's
Heuchera americana - Alumroot
Hibiscus - Rose of Sharon
Hibiscus palustris - Rose Mallow, Swamp
Hieracium aurantiacum - Devil's Paintbrush
Hieracium aurantiacum - Hawkweed, Orange
Hieracium canadense - Hawkweed, Canada
Hieracium gronovii - Hawkweed, Hairy
Hieracium paniculatum - Hawkweed, Panicled
Hieracium pratense - Hawkweed, Field
Hieracium pratense - King Devil
Hieracium scabrum - Hawkweed, Rough

Houstonia caerulea - Bluets
Houstonia caerulea - Innocence
Houstonia caerulea - Quaker Ladies
Houstonia serpyllifolia - Bluets, Creeping
Hyacinthus orientalis - Hyacinth , Common
Hyacinthus orientalis - Hyacinth, Dutch
Hydrangea arborescens - Hydrangea, Wild
Hydrangea petiolaris - Hydrangea, Climbing
Hydrangea quercifolia - Hydrangea, Oak Leaf
Hydrarastis canadensi - Goldenseal
Hydrarastis canadensis - Orangeroot
Hydrophyllum virginianum - Waterleaf, Virginia
Hypericum canadense - St. Johnswort, Canada
Hypericum perforatum - St. Johnswort, Common
Hypericum punctatum - St. Johnswort, Spotted
Hypericum spathulatum - St. Johnswort, Shrubby
Hypoxis hirsuta - Stargrass, Yellow
Ilux - Holly
Impatiens capensis - Touch-me-not, Spotted
Impatiens capensis - Jewelweed
Impatiens pallida - Touch-me-not, Pale
Impatiens pallida - Jewelweed
Iris cristata - Iris, Crested
Iris cristata - Iris, Dwarf Crested
Iris prismatica - Iris, Slender Blue Flag
Iris pseudacorus - Iris, Yellow
Iris verna - Iris, Dwarf
Iris verna - Iris, Vernal
Iris versicolor - Iris, Blue Flag
Iris versicolor - Iris, Larger Blue Flag
Iris versicolor f. murrayada - Iris, Albino Blue Flag
Jeffersonia diphylla - Twinleaf
Kalmia augustifolia - Lambkill
Kalmia augustifolia - Laurel, Sheep
Kalmia latifolia - Laurel, Mountain
Krigia biflora - Cynthia

Lactuca biennis - Lettuce, Tall Blue
Lactuca canadensis - Lettuce, Wild
Lactuca scariola - Lettuce, Prickly
Laportea canadensis - Nettle, Wood
Lapsana communis - Nipplewort
Legumnosae - Caroliniana
Leiophyllum buxifolium - Sand Myrtle
Leontodon autumnalis - Dandelion, Fall
Leonurus cardiaca - Motherwort
Lepidium campestre - Peppergrass, Field
Lespedeza virginica - Clover, Slender Bush
Leucothoe racemosa - Dog Hobble
Liatris - Blazing Star
Liatris graminifolia - Blazing Star, Grass-leaved
Liatris spicata - Blazing Star, Dense
Liatris spicata - Blazing Star, Spiked
Liatris squarrosa - Blazing Star, Scaly
Lilium canadense - Lily, Canada
Lilium canadense - Lily, Meadow
Lilium canadense - Lily, Wild Yellow
Lilium philadelphicum - Lily, Wood
Lilium superbum - Lily, Turk's-cap
Linaria canadensis - Toadflax, Blue
Linaria vulgaris - Butter-and-eggs
Linum perenne lewisii - Flax, Blue
Liriodendron tulipifera - Tuliptree, Yellow-poplar
Lobelia inflata - Indian Tobacco
Lobelia kalmii - Lobelia, Brook
Lobelia kalmii - Lobelia, Kalm's
Lobelia nuttallii - Lobelia Nuttall's
Lobelia siphilitica - Lobelia, Great
Lobelia siphilitica - Lobelia, Great Blue
Lobelia siphilitica f. albiflora - Lobelia, Great White
Lobelia spicata - Lobelia, Spiked
Lobelias cardinalis - Cardinal Flower
Lonicera bella - Honeysuckle, Hybrid of Morrow's and

Tartarian
Lonicera canadensis - Honeysuckle, American Fly
Lonicera morrowi - Honeysuckle, Morrow's
Lonicera sempervirens - Honeysuckle, Coral
Lonicera sempervirens - Honeysuckle, Trumpet
Lonicera tatarica - Honeysuckle, Tartarian
Lotus corniculatus - Birdsfoot Trefoil
Lupinus perennis - Lupine, Wild
Lupinus polyphyllus - Lupine, Garden
Lychnis alba - Campion, White
Lychnis flos-cuculi - Cuckooflower
Lychnis flos-cuculi - Ragged Robin
Lycopus americanus - Horehound, Water
Lycopus unifloris - Bugleweed, Northern
Lyonia mariana - Staggerbush
Lysimachia ciliata - Loosestrife, Fringed
Lysimachia quadrifolia - Loosestrife, Four-leaved
Lysimachia quadrifolia - Loosestrife, Whorled
Lysimachia terrestris - Loosestrife, Yellow
Lysimachia terrestris - Swamp Candles
Lythrum salicaria - Loosestrife, Purple
Magnolia - Magnolia tree
Maianthemum canadense - Lily-of-the-valley, Wild
Maianthemum canadense - Mayflower, Canada
Malus - Apple
Matricaria chamomilla - Chamomile, Wild
Matricaria matricarioides - Pineapple Weed
Medeola virginiana - Cucumber Root, Indian
Medicago lupulina - Medick Black
Medicago sativa - Alfalfa
Medicago sativa - Lucerne
Melampyrum lineare - Cowwheat
Melilotus alba - Clover, White Sweet
Melilotus officinalis - Clover, Yellow Sweet
Mentha piperita - Peppermint
Mertensia virginica - Bluebells, Virginia

Mertensia virginica - Cowslip, Virginia
Mimulus cardinalis - Monkey Flower, Scarlet
Mimulus guttatus - Monkey Flower, Spotted
Mitella diphylla - Bishop's Cap
Mitella diphylla - Miterwort
Monarda fistulosa - Bergamot, Wild
Monarda punctata - Horsemint
Monarda punctata - Horsemint, Dotted
Monotropa uniflora - Corpse Plant
Monotropa uniflora - Indian Pipe
Myosotis laxa - Forget-me-not, Smaller
Narcissus - Daffodil
Nuphar variegatum - Lily, Cow
Nuphar variegatum - Lily, Yellow Pond
Nuphar variegatum - Spatterdock
Oenothera biennis - Evening Primrose, Common
Oenothera fruticosa - Sundrops
Oenothera perennis - Sundrops, Small
Opuntia humfusa, cactaceae - Cactus, Prickly Pear
Orobanche uniflora - Ghost Pipe
Orobanche uniflora - Cancerroot, One-flowered
Osmorhiza claytoni - Sweet Cicely
Oxalis europaea - Sorrel, Yellow Wood
Oxalis montana - Sorrel, Common Wood
Panax trifolius - Ginseng, Dwarf
Papaver - Poppy
Parnassia glauca - Grass-of-Parnassus
Parthenium integrifolium - Feverfew, American
Parthenium integrifolium - Quinine, Wild
Pastinaca sativa - Parsnip, Wild
Pedicularis canadensis - Betony, Wood
Pedicularis canadensis - Lousewort
Penstemon - Beardtongue
Penstemon canescens - Beardtongue, Gray
Penstemon digitalis - Beardtongue, Foxglove
Penstemon digitalis - Beardtongue, White

Penstemon grandiflorus - Beardtongue, Great
Penstemon hirsultus - Beardtongue, Hairy
Phlox bifida - Phlox, Cleft
Phlox bifida - Phlox, Sand
Phlox divaricata - Phlox, Wild Blue
Phlox ovata - Phlox, Mountain
Phlox ozarkiensis - Phlox, Ozark
Phlox pilosa - Phlox, Downy
Phlox subulata - Pink, Ground
Phlox subulata - Pink, Moss
Phlox, stolonifera - Phlox, Creeping
Phlox subulata - Phlox, Moss
Physostegia virginiana - Dragonhead, False
Physotegia virginiana - Obedient Plant
Phytolacca americana - Pokeweed
Podophyllum peltatum - Mandrake
Podophyllum peltatum - Mayapple
Polemonium reptans - Valerian, Greek
Polemonium van-bruntiae - Jacob's Ladder
Polygala paucifolia - Gaywings
Polygala paucifolia - Polygala, Fringed
Polygala paucifolia - Wintergreen, Flowering
Polygala sanguinea - Milkwort, Purple
Polygonatum canaliculatum - Solomon's Seal, Great
Polygonatum pubescens - Solomon's Seal, Hairy
Polygonum amphibium - Smartweed, Water
Polygonum coccineum - Smartweed, Swamp
Polygonum convolvulus - Bindweed, Black
Polygonum hydropiper - Smartweed, Common
Polygonum hydropiper - Water Pepper
Polygonum lapathifolium - Smartweed, Dock-leaved
Polygonum lapathifolium - Smartweed, Nodding
Polygonum lapathifolium - Smartweed, Pale
Polygonum pensylvanicum - Knotweed, Pink
Polygonum pensylvanicum - Pinkweed
Polygonum persicaria - Lady's Thumb

Polygonum sagittatum - Tearthumb, Arrow-leaved
Potentilla argentea - Cinquefoil, Silvery
Potentilla canadensis - Cinquefoil, Dwarf
Potentilla fruiticosa - Cinquefoil, Shrubby
Potentilla norvegica - Cinquefoil, Rough
Potentilla recta - Cinquefoil, Rough-fruited
Potentilla recta - Cinquefoil, Sulphur
Potentilla simplex - Cinquefoil, Common
Prenanthes alba - Lettuce, White
Prenanthes altissima - Lettuce, Tall White
Prenanthes boottii - Rattlesnake Root, Boot's
Prenanthes trifoliata - Gall-of-the-earth
Prenanthes trifoliata - Lion's Foot
Prenanthes trifoliata - Rattlesnake Root, Tall
Prunella vulgaris - Heal-all
Prunella vulgaris - Selfheal
Prunus pensylvanica - Cherry, Bird
Prunus pensylvanica - Cherry, Fire
Prunus pensylvanica - Cherry, Pin
Prunus virginiena - Chokecherry
Pycnanthemum tenuifolium - Mountain Mint, Narrow-leaved
Pycnanthemum virginianum - Mountain Mint, Virginia
Hieracium pilosella - Mouse Ear
Pyrola elliptica - Shinleaf
Pyrus arbutifolia - Chokeberry, Red
Pyrus florabunda - Chokeberry, Purple
Pyxidanthera barbulata - Pixie Moss
Ranunculus - Buttercup
Ranunculus abortivus - Crowfoot, Small-flowered
Ranunculus recurvatus - Crowfoot, Hooked
Ratibida pinnata - Coneflower, Gray-headed
Rhexia virginica - Deergrass
Rhexia virginica - Meadow Beauty
Rhododendron - Azalea
Rhododendron - Rhododendron
Rhododendron arborescens - Azalea, Smooth

Rhododendron calendulaceum - Azalea, Flame
Rhododendron nudiflorum - Azalea, Pink
Rhododendron nudiflorum - Pinxter Flower
Rhododendron vaseyi - Azalea, Pinkshell
Rhododendron viscosum - Azalea, Clammy
Rhododendron viscosum - Honeysuckle, Swamp
Rhus glabra - Sumac, Staghorn
Ribes americanum - Currant, Wild Black
Rosa blanda - Rose, Smooth
Rosa multiflora - Rose, Multiflora
Rosa palustris - Rose, Swamp
Rosa rugosa - Rose, Rugosa
Rosa setigera - Rose, Climbing
Rubus allegheniensis - Blackberry, Common
Rubus flagellaris - Dewberry
Rubus hispidus - Dewberry, Swamp
Rubus occidentalis - Raspberry, Black
Rubus occidentalis - Thimbleberry
Rubus odoratus - Raspberry, Purple-flowering
Rubus pubescens - Raspberry, Dwarf
Rudbeckia laciniata - Coneflower, Green-headed
Rudbeckia laciniata - Coneflower, Tall
Rudbeckia serotina - Black-eyed Susan
Rudbeckia speciosa - Coneflower, Showy
Rudebecia triloba - Coneflower, Thin-leaved
Rudebeckia hirta - Daisy, Gloriosa
Ruellia humilis - Petunia, Wild
Sabatia dodecandra - Gentian, Plymouth
Salix caprea - Willow, Pussy
Sambucus canadensis - Elder, Common
Sambucus pubens - Elder, Red-berried
Sanguinaria canadensis - Bloodroot
Sanicula gregaria - Snakeroot, Clustered
Saponaria officinalis - Soapwort
Saponaria officinalis - Bouncing Bet
Sarracenia purpurea - Pitcher Plant

Satureja vulgaris - Basil, Wild
Saxifraga virginiensis - Saxifrage, Early
Scutellaria incana - Skullcap, Downy
Scutellaria ovata - Skullcap, Heart-leaved
Scutellaria serrata - Skullcap, Showy
Senecio aureus - Groundsel, Golden
Senecio aureus - Ragwort, Golden
Senecio obovatus - Ragwort, Round-leaved
Shortia galacifolia - Oconee Bells
Silene cucubalus - Campion, Bladder
Silene virginica - Pink, Fire
Silphium perfoliatum - Cup Plant
Silphium perfoliatum - Indian Cup
Sisyrinchium - Blue-eyed Grass
Smilacina racemosa - Solomon's Seal, False
Smilacina racemosa - Spikenard, Wild
Smilacina stellata - Solomon's Seal, Star-flowered
Solanum dulcamara - Nightshade, Bittersweet
Solidago - Goldenrod
Solidago bicolor - Silverrod
Solidago caesia - Goldenrod, Blue-stemmed
Solidago caesia - Goldenrod, Wreath
Solidago flexicaulis - Goldenrod, Broad-leaved
Solidago flexicaulis - Goldenrod, Zigzag
Sonchus arvensis - Thistle, Field Sow
Sonchus asper - Thistle, Spiny-leaved Sow
Sonchus oleraceus - Thistle, Common Sow
Spigelia marilandica loganiaceae - Pink, Indian
Spiraea latifolia - Meadowsweet
Spiraea prunifolia - Bridal Wreath
Spiraea tomentosa - Steeplebush
Spiraea tomentosa - Hardhack
Spiranthes cernua - Ladies' Tresses, Autumn
Spiranthes cernua - Ladies' Tresses, Nodding
Stachys tenuifolia - Hedge Nettle, Common
Stellaria graminea - Stitchwort, Lesser

Stellaria pubera - Chickweed, Great
Stellaria pubera - Chickweed, Star
Stokesia laevis - Aster, Stokes Blue
Streptopus reseus - Twisted Stalk, Rose
Streptopus roseus - Mandarin, Rose
Streptopus roseus - Rosybells
Symplocarpus foetidus - Skunk Cabbage
Syringa - Lilac
Tanacetum vulgare - Tansy
Taraxacum officinale - Dandelion, Common
Thalictrum dioicum - Meadow Rue, Early
Thalictrum Polygamum - Meadow Rue, Tall
Thermopsis carolinia - Bushpea
Thlaspi arvense - Pennycress, Field
Thymus serpyllum - Thyme, Wild
Tiarella cordifolia - Foamflower
Tiarella cordifolia - Miterwort, False
Tofieldia glutinosa - Tofieldia, Sticky
Tragopogon pratensis - Goatsbeard, Yellow
Trichostema dichotomum - Blue Curls
Trientalis bocalis - May Star
Trientalis boealis - Starflower
Trifolium agrarium - Clover, Hop
Trifolium agrarium - Clover, Yellow
Trifolium arvense - Clover, Rabbit-foot
Trifolium dubium - Clover, Least Hop
Trifolium pratense - Clover, Red
Trifolium procumbens - Clover, Low Hop
Trifolium repens - Clover, White
Trillium - Trillium
Trillium catesbaei - Trillium, Rose
Trillium cernuum - Trillium, Nodding
Trillium erectum - Birthroot
Trillium erectum - Trillium, Purple
Trillium erectum - Trillium, Red
Trillium erectum - Wake-robin

Trillium erectum F. albiflorum - Trillium, Albino Purple
Trillium grandiflorum - Trillium, Great White
Trillium grandiflorum - Trillium, Large-flowered
Trillium grandiflorum - Trillium, Snow
Trillium grandiflorum - Trillium, White
Trillium lateun - Trillium, Yellow
Trillium ozarkanum - Trillium, Ozark
Trillium recurvatum - Trillium, Prairie
Trillium sessile - Toadshade
Trillium sessile - Trillium, Toad
Trillium viride - Trillium, Green
Trollius laxus - Globeflower
Trollius laxus - Globeflower, Spreading
Tulipa - Tulip
Tussilago farfara - Coltsfoot
Typha - Cattail
Typha latifolia - Cattail, Common
Urtica procera - Nettle, Tall
Uvularia grandiflora - Bellwort, Large-flowered
Uvularia perfoliata - Bellwort
Uvularia sessilifolia - Bellwort, Sessile-leaved
Uvularia sessilifolia - Wild Oats
Uvularia virginianum - Merrybells, Great
Vaccinium augustifolium - Blueberry, Early Low
Vaccinium corymbosum - Blueberry, Highbush
Vaccinium corymbosum - Blueberry, Swamp
Vaccinium oxycoccos - Cranberry, Small
Vaccinium vacillans - Blueberry, Late Low
Valeriana officinalis - Heliotrope, Garden
Valeriana uliginosa - Valerian, Swamp
Vareriana officinalis - Valerian, Garden
Veratrum viride - Hellebore, False
Veratrum viride - Hellebore, White
Verbascum thapsus - Mullein, Common
Verbena hastata - Vervain, Blue
Verbena urticifolia - Vervain, White

Vernonia altissima - Ironweed
Veronica arvensis - Speedwell, Corn
Veronica officinalis - Speedwell, Common
Veronica serpyllifolia - Speedwell, Thyme-leaved
Tradescantia virginiana - Spiderwort
Veratrum viride - Hellebore, False
Veratrum viride - Hellebore, White
Veratrum viride - Indian Poke
Viburnum acerifolium - Dockmackie
Viburnum acerifolium - Viburnum, Maple-leaved
Viburnum alnifolium - Hobblebush
Viburnum nudum - Possum Haw
Viburnum nudum - Withrod, Naked
Viburnum opulus - Cranberry Bush, European
Viburnum sieboldi - Viburnum, Siebold
Viburnum trilobum - Cranberry, Highbush
Viburnum wright - Viburnum, Wright's
Vicia cracca - Vetch, Cow
Vicia cracca - Vetch, Tufted
Vinca minor - Myrtle
Vinca minor - Periwinkle
Viola - Violet
Viola tricolor - Johnny-jump-up
Viola tricolor - Pansy, Field
Weigela - Weigela
Xerophyllum asphodeloides - Turkey Beard
Zizia aptera - Alexanders, Heart-leaved
Zizia aurea - Alexanders, Golden

COMMON-SCIENTIFIC NAME EQUIVALENTS

Adder's Tongue, White - *Erthronium albidum*
Adder's Tongue, Yellow - *Erthronium americanum*
Agrimony - *Agrimonia gryposepala*
Alexanders, Golden - *Zizia aurea*
Alexanders, Heart-leaved - *Zizia aptera*
Alfalfa - *Medicago sativa*
Allegheny Vine - *Adlumia fungosa*
Alumroot - *Heuchera americana*
Alyssum, Hoary - *Berteroa incana*
Anemone, Rue - *Anemonella thalictroides*
Anemone, Tall - *Anemone virginiana*
Anemone, Wood - *Anemone quinquefolia*
Angelica, Great - *Angelica atropurpurea*
Apple - *Malus*
Arbutus, Trailing - *Epigaea regens*
Aster, Aromatic - *Aster oblongifolius*
Aster, Bog - *Aster nemoralis*
Aster, Bristly - *Aster linariifolius*
Aster, Broad-leaved Golden - *Chrysopsis mariana*
Aster, Bushy - *Aster dumosus*
Aster, Calico - *Aster lateriflorus*
Aster, Cape Golden - *Chrysopsis fakcata*
Aster, Flat-topped - *Aster umbellatus*
Aster, Heart-leaved - *Aster cordifolius*
Aster, Heath - *Aster pilosus*
Aster, Large-leaved - *Aster macrophyllus*
Aster, Late Purple - *Aster patens*
Aster, Lowrie's - *Aster lowrieanus*
Aster, Many-flowered - *Aster ericoides*
Aster, Maryland Golden - *Chrysopsis mariana*
Aster, Mountain - *Aster acuminatus*
Aster, New England - *Aster novae-angliae*
Aster, New York - *Aster novi-belgii*
Aster, Panicled - *Aster simplex*

Aster, Prairie Golden - *Chrysopsis villosa*
Aster, Purple-stemmed - *Aster puniceus*
Aster, Schreber's - *Aster schreberi*
Aster, Sharp-leaved - *Aster acuminatus*
Aster, Showy - *Aster spectabilis*
Aster, Sickle-leaved Golden - *Chrysopsis falcata*
Aster, Small White - *Aster vimineus*
Aster, Smooth - *Aster laevis*
Aster, Spreading - *Aster patens*
Aster, Starved - *Aster lateriflorus*
Aster, Stiff - *Aster linariifolius*
Aster, Stokes Blue - *Stokesia laevis*
Aster, Upland - *Aster ptarmicoides*
Aster, Upland White - *Aster ptarmicoides*
Aster, Wavy-leaved - *Aster undulatus*
Aster, White Wood - *Aster divaricatus*
Aster, Whorled - *Aster acuminatus*
Aster, Wood - *Aster divaricatus*
Avens, Cream-colored - *Geum virginianum*
Avens, Purple - *Geum rivale*
Avens, Water - *Geum rivale*
Avens, White - *Geum canadense*
Avens, Yellow - *Geum aleppicum*
Axseed - *Coronilla varia*
Azalea - *Rhododendron*
Azalea, Clammy - *Rhododendron viscosum*
Azalea, Flame - *Rhododendron calendulaceum*
Azalea, Pink - *Rhododendron nudiflorum*
Azalea, Pinkshell - *Rhododendron vaseyi*
Azalea, Smooth - *Rhododendron arborescens*
Bachelor's Button - *Centaurea cyanus*
Balsam Apple, Wild - *Echinocystis lobata*
Baneberry - *Actaea*
Baneberry, Red - *Actaea rubra*
Baneberry, White - *Actaea pachypoda*
Basil, Wild - *Satureja vulgaris*

Beardtongue - *Penstemon*
Beardtongue, Foxglove - *Penstemon digitalis*
Beardtongue, Gray - *Penstemon canescens*
Beardtongue, Great - *Penstemon grandiflorus*
Beardtongue, Hairy - *Penstemon hirsultus*
Beardtongue, White - *Penstemon digitalis*
Bedstraw, Sweet-scented - *Galium triflorum*
Beggar Ticks - *Bidens frondosa*
Bellwort - *Uvularia perfoliata*
Bellwort, Large-flowered - *Uvularia grandiflora*
Bellwort, Sessile-leaved - *Uvularia sessilifolia*
Bergamot, Wild - *Monarda fistulosa*
Betony, Wood - *Pedicularis canadensis*
Bindweed, Black - *Polygonum convolvulus*
Bindweed, Hedge - *Convolvulus sepium*
Bird's Nest - *Daucus carota*
Birdsfoot Trefoil - Lotus corniculatus
Birthroot - *Trillium erectum*
Bishop's Cap - *Mitella diphylla*
Blackberry, Common - *Rubus allegheniensis*
Black-eyed Susan - *Rudbeckia serotina*
Blanket Flower - *Gaillardia*
Blazing Star - *Chamaelirium luteum*
Blazing Star - *Liatris*
Blazing Star, Dense - *Liatris spicata*
Blazing Star, Grass-leaved - *Liatris graminifolia*
Blazing Star, Scaly - *Liatris squarrosa*
Blazing Star, Spiked - *Liatris spicata*
Bleeding Heart, Wild - *Dicentra eximia*
Bloodroot - *Sanguinaria canadensis*
Blue Curls - *Trichostema dichotomum*
Bluebead - *Clintonia borealis*
Bluebell - *Campanula rotundifolia*
Bluebells, Virginia - *Mertensia virginica*
Blueberry, Early Low - *Vaccinium angustifolium*
Blueberry, Highbush - *Vaccinium corymbosum*

Blueberry, Late Low - *Vaccinium vacillans*
Blueberry, Swamp - *Vaccinium corymbosum*
Blue-eyed Grass - *Sisyrinchium*
Bluestar - *Amsonia tabernaemontana*
Bluets - *Houstonia caerulea*
Bluets, Creeping - *Houstonia serpyllifolia*
Blueweed - *Echium vulgare*
Boneset - *Eupatorium perfoliatum*
Boneset, Round-leaved - *Eupatorium rotundifolium*
Bouncing Bet - *Saponaria officinalis*
Bowman's Root - *Gillenia*
Bridal Wreath - *Spiraea prunifolia*
Bugle - *Ajuga reptans*
Bugleweed, Northern - *Lycopus unifloris*
Bugloss, Viper's - *Echium vulgare*
Bur Marigold, Larger - *Bidens laevis*
Burdock, Common - *Arctium minus*
Burning Bush - *Euonymus atropurpureus*
Bushpea - *Thermopsis carolinia*
Butter-and-eggs - *Linaria vulgaris*
Buttercup - *Ranunculus*
Butterfly Weed - *Asclepias tuberosa*
Cactus, Prickly Pear - *Opuntia humfusa, cactaceae*
Campion, Bladder - *Silene cucubalus*
Campion, White - *Lychnis alba*
Cancerroot, One-flowered - *Orobanche uniflora*
Cardinal Flower - *Lobelias cardinalis*
Caroliniana - *Legumnosae*
Carrot, Wild - *Daucus carota*
Catfoot - *Gnaphalium obtusifolium*
Cattail - *Typha*
Cattail, Common - *Typha latifolia*
Celandine - *Chelidonium majus*
Chamomile, Wild - *Matricaria chamomilla*
Cherry, Bird - *Prunus pensylvanica*
Cherry, Fire - *Prunus pensylvanica*

Cherry, Pin - *Prunus pensylvanica*
Chickweed, Great - *Stellaria pubera*
Chickweed, Mouse-ear - *Cerastium vulgatum*
Chickweed, Star - *Stellaria pubera*
Chicory - *Cichorium intybus*
Chokeberry, Purple - *Pyrus florabunda*
Chokeberry, Red - *Pyrus arbutifolia*
Chokecherry - *Prunus virginiena*
Chrysanthemum - *Chrysanthemum*
Cinquefoil, Common - *Potentilla simplex*
Cinquefoil, Dwarf - *Potentilla canadensis*
Cinquefoil, Rough - *Potentilla norvegica*
Cinquefoil, Rough-fruited - *Potentilla recta*
Cinquefoil, Shrubby - *Potentilla fruiticosa*
Cinquefoil, Silvery - *Potentilla argentea*
Cinquefoil, Sulphur - *Potentilla recta*
Clematis - *Clematis*
Clintonia, Yellow - *Clintonia borealis*
Clover, Hop - *Trifolium agrarium*
Clover, Least Hop -*Trifolium dubium*
Clover, Low Hop - *Trifolium procumbens*
Clover, Rabbit-foot - *Trifolium arvense*
Clover, Red - *Trifolium pratense*
Clover, Slender Bush - *Lespedeza virginica*
Clover, White - *Trifolium repens*
Clover, White Sweet - *Melilotus alba*
Clover, Yellow - *Trifolium agrarium*
Clover, Yellow Sweet - *Melilotus officinalis*
Cohosh, Black - *Cimicifuga racemosa*
Cohosh, Blue - *Caulophyllum thalictroides*
Colicroot - *Aletris farinosa*
Coltsfoot - *Tussilago farfara*
Columbine, Wild - *Aquilegia canadensis*
Coneflower, Gray-headed - *Ratibida pinnata*
Coneflower, Green-headed - *Rudbeckia laciniata*
Coneflower, Purple - *Echinacea purpurea*

Coneflower, Showy - *Rudbeckia speciosa*
Coneflower, Tall - *Rudbeckia laciniata*
Coneflower, Thin-leaved - *Rudebecia triloba*
Coreopsis, Eared - *Coreopsis ariculata*
Coreopsis, Lance-leaved - *Coreopsis lancelata*
Coreopsis, Rose - *Coreopsis rosea*
Corpse Plant - *Monotropa uniflora*
Corydalis, Pale - *Corydalis sempervirens*
Corydalis, Pink - *Corydalis sempervirens*
Cosmos - *Cosmos*
Cowslip - *Caltha palustris*
Cowslip, Virginia - *Mertensia virginica*
Cowwheat - *Melampyrum lineare*
Cranberry, Highbush - *Viburnum trilobum*
Cranberry, Small - *Vaccinium oxycoccos*
Cranberry Bush, European - *Viburnum opulus*
Cranesbill, Spotted - *Geranium maculatum*
Crinkleroot - *Dentaria diphylla*
Crowfoot, Hooked - *Ranunculus recurvatus*
Crowfoot, Small-flowered - *Ranunculus abortivus*
Cuckooflower - *Cardamine pratenses*
Cuckooflower - *Lychnis flos-cuculi*
Cucumber, Wild - *Echinocystis lobata*
Cucumber Root, Indian - *Medeola virginiana*
Cup Plant - *Silphium perfoliatum*
Currant, Wild Black - *Ribes americanum*
Cynthia - *Krigia biflora*
Daffodil - *Narcissus*
Daisy, Gloriosa - *Rudebeckia hirta*
Daisy, Oxeye - *Chrysanthemum leucanthemum*
Dandelion, Common - *Taraxacum officinale*
Dandelion, Fall - *Leontodon autumnalis*
Deergrass - *Rhexia virginica*
Devil's Bit - *Chamaelirium luteum*
Devil's Paintbrush - *Hieracium aurantiacum*
Dewberry - *Rubus flagellaris*

Dewberry, Swamp - *Rubus hispidus*
Dittany - *Cunila origanoides*
Dockmackie - *Viburnum acerifolium*
Dog Hobble - *Leucothoe racemosa*
Dogbane, Spreading - *Apocynun androsa emifolium*
Dogwood, Alternate-leaved - *Cornus alternifolia*
Dogwood, Flowering - *Cornus florida*
Dogwood, Gray - *Cornus racemosa*
Dogwood, Japanese - *Cornus kousa*
Dogwood, Korean - *Cornus kousa*
Dogwood, Kousa - *Cornus kousa*
Dogwood, Panicled - *Cornus racemosa*
Dogwood, Red-osier - *Cornus Solonifera*
Dogwood, Silky - *Cornus amomum*
Doll's Eyes - *Actaea pachypoda*
Dragonhead, False - *Physostegia virginiana*
Dutchman's Breeches - *Dicentra*
Elder, Common - *Sambucus canadensis*
Elder, Red-berried - *Sambucus pubens*
Evening Primrose, Common - *Oenothera biennis*
Everlasting, Pearly - *Anaphalis margaritacea*
Everlasting, Sweet - *Gnaphalium obtusifolium*
Fairy Wand - *Chamaelirium luteum*
False Foxglove, Smooth - *Gerdardia flava*
Feverfew, American - *Parthenium integrifolium*
Fireweed - *Epilobium augustifolium*
Flax, Blue - *Linum perenne lewisii*
Fleabane, Common - *Erigeron philadelphicus*
Fleabane, Daisy - *Erigeron annuus*
Fleabane, Lesser Daisy - *Erigeron strigosus*
Fleabane, Philadelphia - *Erigeron philadelphicus*
Fly Poison - *Amianthium muscaetoxicum*
Foamflower - *Tiarella cordifolia*
Forget-me-not, Smaller - *Myosotis laxa*
Fumitory, Climbing - *Adlumia fungosa*
Gall-of-the-earth - *Prenanthes trifoliata*

Gaywings - *Polygala paucifolia*
Gentian, Bottle - *Gentiana clausa*
Gentian, Closed - *Gentiana clausa*
Gentian, Fringed - *Gentiana crinita*
Gentian, Narrow-leaved - *Gentiana linearis*
Gentian, Pine Barren - *Gentiana autumnalis*
Gentian, Plymouth - *Sabatia dodecandra*
Gentian, Striped - *Gentiana villosa*
Geranium, Wild - *Geranium maculatum*
Gerardia, Purple - *Gerardia purpurea*
Ghost Pipe - *Orobanche uniflora*
Gill-over-the-ground - *Glechoma hederacea*
Ginger, Wild - *Asarum canadense*
Ginseng, Dwarf - *Panax trifolius*
Globeflower - *Trollius laxus*
Globeflower, Spreading - *Trollius laxus*
Goatsbeard, Yellow - *Tragopogon pratensis*
Golden Star - *Chrysogonum virginianum*
Goldenrod - *Solidago*
Goldenrod, Blue-stemmed - *Solidago caesia*
Goldenrod, Broad-leaved - *Solidago flexicaulis*
Goldenrod, Wreath - *Solidago caesia*
Goldenrod, Zigzag - *Solidago flexicaulis*
Goldenseal - *Hydrarastis canadensis*
Goldthread - *Coptis groenlandica*
Grass Pink - *Calopogon pulchellus*
Grass Pink Orchid - *Calopogon pulchellus*
Grass-of-Parnassus - *Parnassia glauca*
Ground Ivy - *Glechoma hederacea*
Groundsel, Golden - *Senecio aureus*
Hardhack - *Spiraea tomentosa*
Harebell - *Campanula rotundifolia*
Hawksbeard, Smooth - *Crepis capillaris*
Hawkweed, Canada - *Hieracium canadense*
Hawkweed, Field - *Hieracium pratense*
Hawkweed, Hairy - *Hieracium gronovii*

Hawkweed, Orange - *Hieracium aurantiacum*
Hawkweed, Panicled - *Hieracium paniculatum*
Hawkweed, Rough - *Hieracium scabrum*
Hawthorn - *Crataegus*
Heal-all - *Prunella vulgaris*
Heather - *Calluna vulgaris*
Hedge Nettle, Common - *Stachys tenuifolia*
Heliotrope, Garden - *Valeriana officinalis*
Hellebore, False - *Veratrum viride*
Hellebore, White - *Veratrum viride*
Helleborine - *Epipactis helleborine*
Hemp, Indian - *Apocynum cannabinum*
Hepatica, Round-lobed - *Hepatica americana*
Hepatica, Sharp-lobed - *Hepatica acutiloba*
Herb Robert - *Geranium robertianum*
Hobblebush - *Viburnum alnifolium*
Hog Peanut - *Amphicarpa bracteata*
Holly - *Ilux*
Honewort - *Cryptotaenia canadensis*
Honeysuckle, American Fly - *Lonicera canadensis*
Honeysuckle, Bush - *Diervilla lonicera*
Honeysuckle, Coral - *Lonicera sempervirens*
Honeysuckle, Hybrid of Morrow's and Tartarian - *Lonicera bella*
Honeysuckle, Morrow's - *Lonicera morrowi*
Honeysuckle, Swamp - *Rhododendron viscosum*
Honeysuckle, Tartarian - *Lonicera tatarica*
Honeysuckle, Trumpet - *Lonicera sempervirens*
Horehound, Water - *Lycopus americanus*
Horse Balm - *Collinsonia canadensis*
Horsemint - *Monarda punctata*
Horsemint, Dotted - *Monarda punctata*
Horseradish - *Armoracia lapathifolia*
Horseweed - *Erigeron canadensis*
Hyacinth , Common - *Hyacinthus orientalis*
Hyacinth, Dutch - *Hyacinthus orientalis*

Hydrangea, Climbing - *Hydrangea petiolaris*
Hydrangea, Oak Leaf - *Hydrangea quercifolia*
Hydrangea, Wild - *Hydrangea arborescens*
Indian Cup - *Silphium perfoliatum*
Indian Physic - *Gillenia*
Indian Pipe - *Monotropa uniflora*
Indian Poke - *Veratrum viride*
Indian Tobacco - *Lobelia inflata*
Indian Turnip - *Arisaema atrorubens*
Innocence - *Houstonia caerulea*
Iris, Albino Blue Flag - *Iris versicolor f. murrayada*
Iris, Blue Flag - *Iris versicolor*
Iris, Crested - *Iris cristata*
Iris, Dwarf - *Iris verna*
Iris, Dwarf Crested - *Iris cristata*
Iris, Larger Blue Flag - *Iris versicolor*
Iris, Slender Blue Flag - *Iris prismatica*
Iris, Vernal - *Iris verna*
Iris, Yellow - *Iris pseudacorus*
Ironweed - *Vernonia altissima*
Jack-in-the-pulpit - *Arisaema*
Jacob's Ladder - *Polemonium van-bruntiae*
Jewelweed - *Impatiens capensis*
Joe-Pye Weed, Spotted - *Eupatorium maculatum*
Johnny-jump-up -*Viola tricolor*
King Devil - *Hieracium pratense*
Knapweed, Spotted - *Centaurea maculosa*
Knotweed, Pink - *Polygonum pensylvanicum*
Ladies' Tresses, Autumn - *Spiranthes cernua*
Ladies' Tresses, Nodding - *Spiranthes cernua*
Lady's Slipper, Larger Yellow - *Cypripedium calceolus pubescens*
Lady's Slipper, Pink - *Cypripedium acaule*
Lady's Slipper, Smaller Yellow - *Cypripedium calceolus parviflorum*
Lady's Smock - *Cardamine pratenses*

Lady's Thumb - *Polygonum persicaria*
Lambkill - *Kalmia augustifolia*
Laurel, Mountain - *Kalmia latifolia*
Laurel, Sheep - *Kalmia augustifolia*
Leatherleaf - *Chamaedaphne calyculata*
Leek, Wild - *Allium tricoccum*
Lettuce, Prickly - *Lactuca scariola*
Lettuce, Tall Blue - *Lactuca biennis*
Lettuce, Tall White - *Prenanthes altissima*
Lettuce, White - *Prenanthes alba*
Lettuce, Wild - *Lactuca canadensis*
Lilac - *Syringa*
Lily, Canada - *Lilium canadense*
Lily, Cow - *Nuphar variegatum*
Lily, Day - *Hemerocallis Fulva*
Lily, Meadow - *Lilium canadense*
Lily, Trout - *Erythronium americanum*
Lily, Turk's-cap - *Lilium superbum*
Lily, White Trout - *Erythronium albidum*
Lily, Wild Yellow - *Lilium canadense*
Lily, Wood - *Lilium philadelphicum*
Lily, Yellow Pond - *Nuphar variegatum*
Lily-of-the-valley, Wild - *Maianthemum canadense*
Ling - *Calluna vulgaris*
Lion's Foot - *Prenanthes trifoliata*
Liverleaf - *Hepatica americana*
Lobelia, Brook - *Lobelia kalmii*
Lobelia, Great - *Lobelia siphilitica*
Lobelia, Great Blue - *Lobelia siphilitica*
Lobelia, Great White - *Lobelia siphilitica f. albiflora*
Lobelia, Kalm's - *Lobelia kalmii*
Lobelia Nuttall's - *Lobelia nuttallii*
Lobelia, Spiked - *Lobelia spicata*
Loosestrife, Four-leaved - *Lysimachia quadrifolia*
Loosestrife, Fringed - *Lysimachia ciliata*
Loosestrife, Purple - *Lythrum salicaria*

Loosestrife, Whorled - *Lysimachia quadrifolia*
Loosestrife, Yellow - *Lysimachia terrestris*
Lousewort - *Pedicularis canadensis*
Lucerne - *Medicago sativa*
Lupine, Garden - *Lupinus polyphyllus*
Lupine, Wild - *Lupinus perennis*
Madder, Wild - *Galium mollugo*
Magnolia tree - *Magnolia*
Mallow, Poppy - *Callirhoe triangulata*
Mallow, Poppy - *Callirhoe involucrata*
Mallow, Poppy - *Callirhoe digitata*
Mandarin, Rose - *Streptopus roseus*
Mandrake - *Podophyllum peltatum*
Maple, Striped - *Acer pensylvanicum*
Marigold, Marsh - *Caltha palustris*
May Star - *Trientalis bocalis*
Mayapple - *Podophyllum peltatum*
Mayflower - *Epigaea repens*
Mayflower, Canada - *Maianthemum canadense*
Meadow Beauty - *Rhexia virginica*
Meadow Rue, Early - *Thalictrum dioicum*
Meadow Rue, Tall - *Thalictrum Polygamum*
Meadowsweet - *Spiraea latifolia*
Medick, Black - *Medicago lupulina*
Merrybells, Great - *Uvularia virginianum*
Milfoil - *Achillea millefolium*
Milkweed, Common - *Asclepias syriaca*
Milkweed, Purple - *Asclepias purpurascens*
Milkweed, Swamp - *Asclepias incarnata*
Milkwort, Purple - *Polygala sanguinea*
Mistflower - *Eupatorium coelestinum*
Miterwort - *Mitella diphylla*
Miterwort, False - *Tiarella cordifolia*
Moccasin Flower - *Cypripedium acaule*
Monkey Flower - *Mimulus ringens*
Monkey Flower, Scarlet - *Mimulus cardinalis*

Monkey Flower, Spotted - *Mimulus guttatus*
Monkshood, Wild - *Aconitum uncinatum*
Motherwort - *Leonurus cardiaca*
Mountain Fringe - *Adlumia fungosa*
Mountain Mint, Narrow-leaved - *Pycnanthemum tenuifolium*
Mountain Mint, Virginia - *Pycnanthemum virginianum*
Mouse Ear - *Hieracium pilosella*
Mullein, Common - *Verbascum thapsus*
Mustard, Garlic - *Alliaria officinalis*
Mustard, Tower - *Arabis glabra*
Mustard, Treacle - *Erysimum cheiranthoides*
Mustard, Wormseed - *Erysimum cheiranthoides*
Myrtle - *Vinca minor*
Nettle, Hemp - *Galeopsis tetrahit*
Nettle, Tall - *Urtica procera*
Nettle, Wood - *Laportea canadensis*
Nightshade, Bittersweet - *Solanum dulcamara*
Nightshade, Enchanter's - *Circaea quadrisulcata*
Nipplewort - *Lapsana communis*
Obedient Plant - *Physotegia virginiana*
Oconee Bells - *Shortia galacifolia*
Onion, Nodding Wild - *Allium cernuum*
Orangeroot - *Hydrarastis canadensis*
Orchid, Yellow Fringed - *Habenaria ciliaris*
Orchis, Smaller Purple Fringed - *Habenaria psycodes*
Orchis, Yellow Fringed - *Habenaria ciliaris*
Pansy, Field - *Viola tricolor*
Parsley, Hemlock - *Conioselinum chinese*
Parsnip, Wild - *Pastinaca sativa*
Pennycress, Field - *Thlaspi arvense*
Pepperbush, Sweet - *Clethra alnifolia*
Peppergrass, Field - *Lepidium campestre*
Peppermint - *Mentha piperita*
Periwinkle - *Vinca minor*
Petunia, Wild - *Ruellia humilis*
Phlox, Cleft - *Phlox bifida*

Phlox, Creeping - *Phlox, stolonifera*
Phlox, Downy - *Phlox pilosa*
Phlox, Moss - *Phlox subulata*
Phlox, Mountain - *Phlox ovata*
Phlox, Ozark - *Phlox ozarkiensis*
Phlox, Sand - *Phlox bifida*
Phlox, Wild Blue - *Phlox divaricata*
Pineapple Weed -*Matricaria matricarioides*
Pink - *Dianthus*
Pink, Deptford - *Dianthus armeria*
Pink, Fire - *Silene virginica*
Pink, Ground - *Phlox subulata*
Pink, Indian - *Spigelia marilandica loganiaceae*
Pink, Maiden - *Dianthus deltoides*
Pink, Moss - *Phlox subulata*
Pink, Swamp - *Helonias bullata*
Pinkweed - *Polygonum pensylvanicum*
Pinxter Flower - *Rhododendron nudiflorum*
Pitcher Plant - *Sarracenia purpurea*
Pixie Moss - *Pyxidanthera barbulata*
Pleurisy Root - *Asclepias tuberosa*
Pokeweed - *Phytolacca americana*
Polygala, Fringed - *Polygala paucifolia*
Poppy - *Papaver*
Possum Haw - *Virburnum nudum*
Prairie Smoke - *Geum triflorum*
Pussytoes, Field - *Antennaria neglecta*
Pussytoes, Plantain-leaved - *Antennaria plantaginifolia*
Pussytoes, Smaller - *Antennaria neodioica*
Pussytoes, Smooth - *Antennaria parlinii*
Quaker Ladies - *Houstonia caerulea*
Queen Anne's Lace - *Daucus carota*
Quinine, Wild - *Parthenium integrifolium*
Ragged Robin - *Lychnis flos-cuculi*
Ragwort, Golden - *Senecio aureus*
Ragwort, Round-leaved - *Senecio obovatus*

Ramps - *Allium tricoccum*
Raspberry, Black - *Rubus occidentalis*
Raspberry, Dwarf - *Rubus pubescens*
Raspberry, Purple-flowering - *Rubus odoratus*
Rattlesnake Plantain, Downy - *Goodyera pubescens*
Rattlesnake Root, Boot's - *Prenanthes boottii*
Rattlesnake Root, Tall - *Prenanthes trifoliata*
Redbud - *Cercis*
Rhododendron - *Rhododendron*
Richweed - *Collinsonia canadensis*
Robin's Plantain - *Erigeron pulchellus*
Rock Cress, Hairy - *Arabis hirsuta*
Rock Cress, Pink - *Arabis blepharophylla*
Rocket, Dame's - *Hesperis matronalis*
Rocket, Yellow - *Barbarea vulgaris*
Rose, Climbing - *Rosa setigera*
Rose, Multiflora - *Rosa multiflora*
Rose, Rugosa - *Rosa rugosa*
Rose, Smooth - *Rosa blanda*
Rose, Swamp - *Rosa palustris*
Rose Mallow, Swamp - *Hibiscus palustris*
Rose of Sharon - *Hibiscus*
Rosybells - *Streptopus roseus*
Russian-olive shrub - *Elaeagnus augustifolia*
Sand Myrtle - *Leiophyllum buxifolium*
Sandwort, Blunt-leaved - *Arenaria lateriflora*
Sandwort, Grove - *Arenaria laterifolora*
Sarsaparilla, Bristly - *Aralia hispida*
Sarsaparilla, Wild - *Aralia nudicaulis*
Saxifrage, Early - *Saxifraga virginiensis*
Scabious, Sweet - *Erigeron annuus*
Selfheal - *Prunella vulgaris*
Shadbush, Common - *Amelanchier arborea*
Shadbush, Smooth - *Amelanchier laevis*
Shepherd's Purse - *Capsella bursa-pastoris*
Shinleaf - *Pyrola elliptica*

Shooting Star - *Dodecatheon meadia*
Shooting Star, Jewel - *Dodecatheon amethystinum*
Silverrod - *Solidago bicolor*
Skullcap, Downy - *Scutellaria incana*
Skullcap, Heart-leaved - *Scutellaria ovata*
Skullcap, Showy - *Scutellaria serrata*
Skunk Cabbage - *Symplocarpus foetidus*
Smartweed, Common - *Polygonum hydropiper*
Smartweed, Dock-leaved - *Polygonum lapathifolium*
Smartweed, Nodding - *Polygonum lapathifolium*
Smartweed, Pale - *Polygonum lapathifolium*
Smartweed, Swamp - *Polygonum coccineum*
Smartweed, Water - *Polygonum amphibium*
Snakeroot, Black - *Cimicifuga racemosa*
Snakeroot, Clustered - *Sanicula gregaria*
Snakeroot, Sampson's - *Gentiana villosa*
Snakeroot, White - *Eupatorium rugosum*
Sneezeweed - *Helenium autumnale*
Soapwort - *Saponaria officinalis*
Solomon's Seal, False - *Smilacina racemosa*
Solomon's Seal, Great - *Polygonatum canaliculatum*
Solomon's Seal, Hairy - *Polygonatum pubescens*
Solomon's Seal, Star-flowered - *Smilacina stellata*
Sorrel, Common Wood - *Oxalis montana*
Sorrel, Yellow Wood - *Oxalis europaea*
Spatterdock - *Nuphar variegatum*
Speedwell, Common - *Veronica officinalis*
Speedwell, Corn - *Veronica arvensis*
Speedwell, Thyme-leaved -*Veronica serpyllifolia*
Spiderwort - *Tradescantia virginiana*
Spikenard, Wild - *Smilacina racemosa*
Spring Beauty - *Claytonia virginica*
Spring Beauty, Carolina - *Claytonia caroliniana*
Spurge, Cypress - *Euphorbia cyparissias*
Squirrel Corn - *Dicentra cucullaria*
St. Johnswort, Canada - *Hypericum canadense*

St. Johnswort, Common - *Hypericum perforatum*
St. Johnswort, Shrubby - *Hypericum spathulatum*
St. Johnswort, Spotted - *Hypericum punctatum*
Staggerbush - *Lyonia mariana*
Starflower - *Trientalis boealis*
Stargrass, Yellow - *Hypoxis hirsuta*
Steeplebush - *Spiraea tomentosa*
Sticktight - *Bidens frondosa*
Stitchwort, Lesser - *Stellaria graminea*
Stoneroot - *Collinsonia canadensis*
Strawberry - *Fragaria*
Strawberry, Wild - *Fragaria virginiana*
Sumac, Staghorn - *Rhus glabra*
Sundew, Round-leaved - *Drosera rotundifolia*
Sundrops - *Oenothera fruticosa*
Sundrops, Small - *Oenothera perennis*
Sunflower, Pale-leaved - *Helianthus strumosus*
Sunflower, Thin-leaved - *Helianthus decapetalus*
Swamp Candles - *Lysimachia terrestris*
Swamp Hyacinth - *Helonias bullata*
Sweet Cicily - *Osmorhiza claytoni*
Sweet William - *Dianthus barbatus*
Tansy - *Tanacetum vulgare*
Tearthumb, Arrow-leaved - *Polygonum sagittatum*
Thimbleberry - *Rubus occidentalis*
Thimbleweed - *Anemone virginiana*
Thistle, Bull - *Cirsium vulgare*
Thistle, Canada - *Cirsium arvense*
Thistle, Common Sow - *Sonchus oleraceus*
Thistle, Field Sow - *Sonchus arvensis*
Thistle, Spiny-leaved Sow - *Sonchus asper*
Thoroughwort - *Eupatorium perfoliatum*
Thyme, Wild - *Thymus serpyllum*
Tick Trefoil, Dillen's - *Desmodium glabellum*
Tick Trefoil, Naked-flowered - *Desmodium nudiflorum*
Tick Trefoil, Panicled - *Desmodium paniculatum*

Tick Trefoil, Showy - *Desmodium canadense*
Tickseed, Pink - *Coreopsis rosea*
Toadflax, Blue - *Linaria canadensis*
Toadshade - *Trillium sessile*
Tofieldia, Sticky - *Tofieldia glutinosa*
Toothwort - *Dentaria diphylla*
Touch-me-not, Pale - *Inpatiens pallida*
Touch-me-not, Spotted - *Impatiens capensis*
Trillium - *Trillium*
Trillium, Albino Purple - *Trillium erectum F. albiflorum*
Trillium, Great White - *Trillium grandiflorum*
Trillium, Green - *Trillium viride*
Trillium, Large-flowered - *Trillium grandiflorum*
Trillium, Nodding - *Trillium cernuum*
Trillium, Ozark - *Trillium ozarkanum*
Trillium, Prairie - *Trillium recurvatum*
Trillium, Purple - *Trillium erectum*
Trillium, Red - *Trillium erectum*
Trillium, Rose - *Trillium catesbaei*
Trillium, Snow - *Trillium grandiflorum*
Trillium, Toad - *Trillium sessile*
Trillium, White - *Trillium grandiflorum*
Trillium, Yellow - *Trillium lateun*
Tulip - *Tulipa*
Tuliptree, Yellow-poplar - *Liriodendron tulipifera*
Turkey Beard - *Xerophyllum asphodeloides*
Turtlehead - *Chelone glabra*
Turtlehead, Pink - *Chelone lyoni*
Twinleaf - *Jeffersonia diphylla*
Twisted Stalk, Rose - *Streptopus reseus*
Umbrella Leaf - *Diphylleie cymosa*
Valerian, Garden - *Vareriana officinalis*
Valerian, Greek - *Polemonium reptans*
Valerian, Swamp - *Valeriana uliginosa*
Vervain, Blue - *Verbena hastata*
Vervain, White - *Verbena urticifolia*

Vetch, Cow - *Vicia cracca*
Vetch, Crown - *Coronilla varia*
Vetch, Tufted - *Vicia cracca*
Viburnum, Maple-leaved - *Viburnum acerifolium*
Viburnum, Siebold - *Viburnum sieboldi*
Viburnum, Wright's - *Viburnum wright*
Violet - *Viola*
Violet, Dame's - *Hesperis matronalis*
Virgin's Bower - *Clematis virginiana*
Wahoo - *Euonymus atropurpureus*
Wake-robin - *Trillium erectum*
Water Pepper - *Polygonum hydropiper*
Waterleaf, Virginia - *Hydrophyllum virginianum*
Weigela - *Weigela*
Wild Oats - *Uvularia sessilifolia*
Willow, Pussy - *Salix caprea*
Willow Herb, Great - *Epilobium augustifolium*
Willow Herb, Hairy - *Epilobium hirsutum*
Willow Herb, Purple-leaved - *Epilobium coloratum*
Windflower - *Anemone quinquefolia*
Winter Cress, Common - *Barbarea vulgaris*
Wintergreen, Flowering - *Polygala paucifolia*
Wintergreen, Spotted - *Chimaphila maculata*
Wintergreen, Striped - *Chemaphila maculata*
Withrod, Naked - *Viburnum nudum*
Wood Mint, Hairy - *Blephilia hirsuta*
Yarrow - *Achillea millefolium*

A

G

H

T